Mikhail Bulgakov

Twayne's World Authors Series
Russian Literature

Charles Moser, Editor

George Washington University

TWAS 750

MIKHAIL BULGAKOV
(1891–1940)
Photograph courtesy of
Charles Schlacks, Jr., Publisher

Mikhail Bulgakov

By Nadine Natov

George Washington University

Twayne Publishers • Boston

Mikhail Bulgakov

Nadine Natov

Copyright © 1985 by G. K. Hall & Company
All Rights Reserved
Published by Twayne Publishers
A Division of G. K. Hall & Co.
A publishing subsidiary of ITT
70 Lincoln Street
Boston, Massachusetts 02111

Book Production by Elizabeth Todesco

Book Design by Barbara Anderson

Printed on permanent/durable acid-free
paper and bound in the United States of
America.

Library of Congress Cataloging in Publication Data

Natov, Nadine.
   Mikhail Bulgakov.

   (Twayne's world authors series; TWAS 750. Russian literature)
   Bibliography: p. 137
   Includes index.
   1. Bulgakov, Mikhail Afanas'evich, 1891–1940.
2. Authors, Russian—20th century—Biography.
I. Title.   II.   Series: Twayne's world authors series; TWAS 750.
III. Series: Twayne's world authors series. Russian literature.
PG3476.B78Z77 1985   891.78'4209   84–19231
ISBN 0-8057-6598-0

891.7842
B933

Contents

About the Author
Preface
Chronology

117807

About the Author

Nadine Natov was born in Tashkent. She received her undergraduate and graduate degrees from the Moscow Institute of Modern Languages, did graduate work in Russian, French, and comparative literature at the university of Hamburg, the Sorbonne, and Wayne University, and was awarded a Ph.D. at the University of Michigan. Since 1963 she has taught Russian literature and language at George Washington University, where she is now professor of Russian.

Nadine Natov's chief fields of interest are Dostoevsky (since 1971 she has been executive secretary of the International Dostoevsky Society and is currently president of the North American Dostoevsky Society), Turgenev, and modern Russian literature, particularly Mikhail Bulgakov and Yuri Trifonov. She is the author of a number of articles in these fields, and a book, *Dostoevsky in Bad Ems*. She has edited a special issue of *Canadian American Slavic Studies* on Mikhail Bulgakov (1981) and a Dostoevsky commemorative volume of *Transactions* of the Association of Russian-American Scholars in the U.S.A. (1981), and coedited a Turgenev commemorative volume of the *Transactions* (1983).

Preface

Mikhail Bulgakov had a difficult life and a peculiar career. Many details of his life have long been unknown or distorted: for instance, the *Great Soviet Encyclopedia* (1927) claimed that Bulgakov had spent several years in Berlin when in fact he had never been abroad: the Soviet authorities had even denied him permission to go to Paris to see his brothers.

Bulgakov's early stories are scattered in various publications that are difficult to locate. Many of his works were rejected by the publishing houses to which they were submitted, and several of his plays were banned. During his lifetime Bulgakov was known primarily as the author of one play—*The Days of the Turbins*—and of the stage adaptation of Gogol's novel *Dead Souls*. Nearly a quarter of a century after his death, four of Bulgakov's novels were published in the Soviet Union and brought him posthumous fame.

Bulgakov was first introduced to the American reader in 1967 by two translations of his last novel, *The Master and Margarita;* a few years later Ellendea and Carl Proffer translated some of his early stories and plays. Now Bulgakov scholarship is expanding rapidly, and over the last decade numerous articles on him have appeared in English. At the time of this study's completion, only two books on Bulgakov were available—one in Italian, by Eridano Bazzarelli, and one in English, by A. Colin Wright—but several other scholars are working on books about this talented writer.

The present volume is designed as a convenient survey of Bulgakov's life and works, many of which are still unknown even to Russian readers. Space limitations, however, have necessitated the omission of some valuable material, and certain aspects of Bulgakov's works could be touched upon only briefly here. I hope to develop them further in other studies.

The present monograph consists of nine chapters. They contain a survey of Bulgakov's life based on the most recent available material; analysis of his semi-autobiographical works, such as *A Country Doctor's Notebook, Notes on the Cuffs,* "Bohème," some feuilletons and *Theatrical Novel (Notes of a Dead Man),* as well as such early satirical feuilletons and stories as "Diaboliad," "The Fatal Eggs," and *Heart of a Dog.* Special chapters are devoted to his works on the Civil War (the novel *The White Guard* and the plays *The Days of the Turbins* and *Flight*); to the plays *Zoika's Apartment, The Crimson Island, Adam and Eve, Bliss,* and *Ivan Vasil'evich,* two of which were produced in Bulgakov's lifetime; and to his works on Molière (the plays *Half-Witted Jourdain* and *Cabal of Hypocrites* and the novel *Life of Monsieur de Molière*). Bulgakov's greatest work—his "sunset" novel *The Master and Margarita*—is discussed in chapter 7, and his last plays *(Alexander Pushkin,* [*Last Days*], *Don Quixote, Batum),* his stage adaptations, and his opera libretti are the subjects of chapter 8.

I have emphasized the literary value of Bulgakov's works, the variety of his styles, and the ambivalence of many of his characters. Unusual blends of disparate elements—from genuine humor and lyricism to phantasmagoric grotesque and tragedy—demonstrate Bulgakov's artistic power, his capacity to tie together into an impressive whole the complexities of life, and his powerful imagination which created innovative works.

I should like to express here my appreciation to George Washington University for providing me with a summer grant to support my work on this book.

Nadine Natov

George Washington University

Chronology

1927   Works on the play *The Crimson Island* for the Kamerny Theater and on *Flight* for the Art Theater.

1928   11 December, *The Crimson Island* is premiered by the Kamerny Theater. Begins work on what will become *The Master and Margarita*.

1929   June, *The Turbins* is banned; *Zoika's Apartment* and *The Crimson Island* are eliminated from the repertory. 3 September, asks to go abroad temporarily. October, begins the play *A Cabal of Hypocrites*.

1930   February, *A Cabal of Hypocrites* rejected by the Main Repertory Committee. 28 March, sends a letter to the Soviet government. 18 April, called by Stalin, begins to work for the Theater of Working Youth (TRAM) as a literary consultant and for the Moscow Art Theater as assistant producer.

1931   14 March, requests TRAM to relieve him of his position. July, signs a contract with the Leningrad Red Theater and Vakhtangov Theater in Moscow for a play "on the theme of the future war" (*Adam and Eve*). October, a corrected version of the play *A Cabal of Hypocrites* is approved for production under the title *Molière*.

1932   18 February, *The Days of the Turbins* repremieres at the Moscow Art Theater. *Molière* sporadically rehearsed at the Art Theater. Fall, separates from Liubov' Evgenievna. 4 October, marries Elena Sergeevna Shilovskaya. 28 November, stage adaptation of Gogol's *Dead Souls* premiered at the Moscow Art Theater.

1933   Biographical novel on Molière rejected. Works on the play *Bliss*.

1934   Health begins to fail. 1 December, Dickens's *Pickwick Papers* premieres at the Moscow Art Theater; Bulgakov plays the part of the Judge.

1935   Finishes the play *Alexander Pushkin (Last Days)*.

1936   15 February, *Molière* premieres at the Moscow Art Theater, later banned. 13 May, play *Ivan Vasil'evich* banned. 15 September, leaves the Moscow Art Theater and accepts a position with the Bolshoi Opera Theater.

1937   April, reads chapters from *Notes of a Dead Man (Theatrical Novel)* to friends.

1938 23 May, finishes the sixth version of *The Master and Margarita.*

1939 January, begins to write the play *A Pastor (Batum)* for the Moscow Art Theater. August, the play is banned. A doctor confirms the cause of Bulgakov's fading eyesight—hypertonic nephrosclerosis. He loses the ability to read.

1940 10 March, Bulgakov dies at his home. 12 March, body cremated and buried at Novodevich'e cemetery in Moscow.

Chapter One
Life Story

Mikhail Bulgakov's life story may forever remain incomplete, since he left no memoirs, no story of his life, as did his schoolmate Konstantin Paustovsky, nor any extended autobiographical essay, as did Boris Pasternak. We know from his archives that by 1926 Bulgakov had written three notebooks of a diary covering the years 1921–26. After his apartment was searched, Bulgakov abandoned his diary and later destroyed it, preserving only four pages which he later gave to his wife. Since he spent much of the 1930s the victim of a "conspiracy of silence," Bulgakov had no biographer.

Fortunately, Bulgakov had a devoted woman at his side during the last decade of his life. His third wife, Elena Sergeevna, faithfully preserved his archives and manuscripts. And it is to her the writer owes his rise from the ashes after years of neglect, for, when circumstances finally permitted in the mid-1950s, Elena Sergeevna made her husband's manuscripts available for publication.

Bulgakov left only two brief sketches of an autobiography, one written in October 1924, the other on 20 March 1937. These sketches were published in 1966 in Moscow, in a collection of autobiographies of Soviet writers, supplemented by the fragmentary memoirs of Bulgakov's second wife and by those of several of his friends.

The facts of Bulgakov's life should be considered separately from the numerous short stories, feuilletons, and fragments of novels regarded as autobiographical by his friends. These are primarily *Zapiski iunogo vracha (A Country Doctor's Notebook), Zapiski na manzhetakh* (Notes on the cuffs), and *Teatral'nyi roman (Black Snow: A Theatrical Novel),* as well as some passages from *Belaia gvardiia (The White Guard)* and *Master i Margarita (The Master and Margarita).* To be sure, these works can supplement his life story to a certain extent. Bulgakov sometimes used his own experience as the basis for his fiction, frequently in the first person. A careful reading of the foregoing works, some feuilletons and short stories of 1922–24, containing descriptions of contemporary Kiev and Moscow, and

1

several pages of *Zhizn' gospodina de Moliera (Life of Monsieur de Molière)*
make it possible to distinguish, within the fictional narrative, the
author's voice. Indeed, Bulgakov's life story is in itself a fascinating
novel, as we shall see.

Childhood and Youth (1891–1921)

Mikhail Bulgakov was born in Kiev on 15 May 1891 to Afanasy
Ivanovich Bulgakov, a professor at the Kiev Theological Academy,
and his wife, Varvara Mikhailovna, née Pokrovskaya. Mikhail's
grandmother on his mother's side was Anfisa Ivanovna Pokrovskaya,
née Turbina, the name that Mikhail later gave to his favorite
protagonists.

Mikhail's father dedicated himself to the study of the history of
religious reforms, lectured at the Academy on the history of Western
religions, and wrote extensively. In 1926 Bulgakov recalled that
the image of a lamp with a shade was associated in his mind with
his father writing at his desk. For two books published in 1901 and
1906, Afanasy Bulgakov was granted the title of doctor of theology.

There is no doubt that Bulgakov's talks with his father and his
colleagues, as well as frequent visits to the Theological Academy
museum and Kiev's St. Vladimir Cathedral, rich in religious paint-
ings, contributed to his interest in the history of religions and the
Gospel, which found expression in his last novel, *The Master and
Margarita*.

The Bulgakov family was large and happy, consisting of seven
children, of whom Mikhail was the eldest. It was also very musical:
the father played the violin; the mother was an excellent pianist;
and Mikhail played the piano too.

The family changed apartments several times. In 1907 the Bulgakovs rented the second floor of house No. 13 on Andreevsky Hill,
which now has become a historical landmark.

Mikhail received his early education at home. In 1900 he entered
the preparatory class of the Second High School. The next year he
entered the Alexandrovsky (First) High School, the finest school in
Kiev.

Afanasy Bulgakov died in 1907, at the age of forty-eight, from
hypertonic nephrosclerosis, the disease from which Mikhail too would
die. After the death of her husband, Varvara Mikhailovna stayed
with her seven children in the same house, even adding two other

children, her nephews Konstantin and Nikolay. Mikhail was very close to Konstantin—they were the same age and later corresponded frequently. Soon Varvara Mikhailovna began to teach evening courses for women. After her children grew up, she remarried.

Mikhail spent eight years at the Alexandrovsky High School. During that time he was known as an excellent storyteller, with an exceptional talent for brilliant improvisation of funny stories. His schoolmate Konstantin Paustovsky remembered that when boating with his friends on the Dnepr River, Bulgakov would concoct stories in which "reality and fantasy were so closely interwoven that the audience was unable to distinguish where the borderline was."[1]

Soon the theater became Mikhail's favorite entertainment. During his school years, Bulgakov visited Kiev's Majestic Opera House no less than fifty times to listen to his favorite opera, *Faust*. He knew its score by heart, and its sounds are audible in some of his later works—*Belaia gvardiia (The White Guard), Dni Turbinykh (The Days of the Turbins), Teatral'nyi roman (Theatrical Novel),* and *Adam i Eva (Adam and Eve)*. According to his sister, Mikhail often dreamed of becoming an opera singer.

Kiev also had a Ukrainian theater and a Russian drama theater, the Solovtsov Theater, famed as the best provincial theater in Russia. Its repertory was varied and distinguished. Mikhail saw dozens of plays—from Molière and Gogol to Tolstoy, Chekhov, and Gorky. Mikhail was not only an enthusiastic theatergoer; he also composed little humoresques and liked to perform them with members of his family and their friends.

In 1909 Mikhail graduated from high school and enrolled in the medical school of the University of Kiev. Thus, though his mother wished to see all her sons become engineers and his own dream called him to a theatrical career, Mikhail became a physician. At least this profession was also popular in the family. Mikhail passed his final examinations and was certified with distinction on 6 April 1916.[2]

At the time of his graduation Mikhail was twenty-five, and already married. He had met Tatyana (Tasya) Nikolaevna Lappá, four years younger than he, in the summer of 1909, when she came to Kiev from Saratov to visit her aunt, a close friend of Mikhail's mother. The wedding took place on 26 April 1913.

Immediately after his graduation, in 1916, Mikhail started to work in Kiev at one of the hospitals for wounded soldiers; then he served at field hospitals on the Southwestern Front as a volunteer for the Red Cross. In September 1916 he arrived at a one-doctor hospital in the village of Nikolskoe in the Sychov district in the northwestern province of Smolensk, about twenty miles from the nearest railroad station. This hospital was one of many created by local rural councils to provide medical services for the peasantry. Frequently Mikhail had to perform complex operations although he was not trained for difficult surgical cases.

Mikhail stayed in Nikolskoe until 18 September 1917. When he left, he was characterized as "indefatigable."[3] According to his wife Tatyana, when her husband once became infected while treating a diphtheria patient, he had terrible pains that could be alleviated only by morphine, and for a certain time became a morphine addict.[4]

From Nikolskoe Mikhail transferred to the city hospital in Vyazma, where living and working conditions were much better. But he made repeated attempts to get to Kiev or Moscow. At the time he wrote his sister Nadezhda, who was then living in Czarskoe Selo near Petrograd: "I am again toiling here, in Vyazma. . . . I live in complete loneliness. . . . I find consolation only in my work and in my readings at night. . . . I am so anxious to leave here for Moscow or Kiev. . . . The New Year will come in two hours. What will it bring to me?[5] On 19 February 1918 Mikhail went once more to Moscow, and this time received permission to relocate.

Thus, at the end of February 1918 Mikhail returned to Kiev, where he spent the remaining months of 1918 and the year 1919 with his family in the cozy apartment on Andreevsky Hill. He equipped one room as an office and began to practice as a venerologist.

Mikhail's brief sojourn in Kiev coincided with the most troubled time in the life of the city. After the abdication of Emperor Nicholas II in March 1917, the Ukrainian Central Rada took power in Kiev and, in November 1917, proclaimed the independence of the Ukrainian People's Republic. The Rada's rule was overthrown by Bolshevik troops entering Kiev at the beginning of February 1918. Then on 24 February 1918, German troops entered the Ukraine, ousted the Bolsheviks, and in March extended their authority to Kiev. At first the Germans supported the Ukrainian Central Rada. But later, because of a conflict between the Rada and German military authorities, the Germans decided to support a new government, created on 29 April 1918, and headed by a former czarist general, Pavel Skoropadsky, who was proclaimed Hetman of all the Ukraine.

Mikhail Bulgakov witnessed the German withdrawal from Kiev in December 1918, the collapse of Skoropadsky's government, and the seizure of Kiev by the Ukrainian Nationalist Army, commanded by Simon Petliura, who held Kiev for six weeks. Early in February 1919 Petliura withdrew under pressure of Red troops, who were in turn ousted in August 1919 by General Anton Denikin's Volunteer Army ("White Army"). Denikin held Kiev until 16 December 1919, when he was defeated by the Red Army. But the extremely complex struggle for power among diverse forces continued until the summer of 1920.

Toward the end of Hetman Skoropadsky's rule, Mikhail served in a hospital located in the center of the city. Petliura's military authorities mobilized Mikhail as their regimental doctor, but he escaped when Petliura's troops began their retreat on 3 February 1919.

While Mikhail practiced medicine in the midst of chaos, his brothers Nikolay and Ivan fought in the battles around their native city. Later on, like their cousins Konstantin and Nikolay, they left Kiev with the units of the Russian Volunteer Army.

In September 1919, while Kiev was ruled by General Anton Denikin's army, the Bulgakov family received its first news from Konstantin, who was serving in the Caucasus. Hoping to find traces of his brothers Nikolay and Ivan, Mikhail decided to go to the south of Russia as a field physician in the Third Kazak Regiment. There the battles continued, and Mikhail was unable to find his brothers, both of whom had been wounded and who later left for Rumania. At the end of December 1919, Mikhail resigned from the military service in Vladikavkaz.

This action opened a new period in Bulgakov's life. In February 1920, Mikhail had just begun his affiliation with the newspaper *Kavkaz* (Caucasus), edited by the experienced journalist Nikolay Pokrovsky, when the paper was shut down after Soviet rule was established in Vladikavkaz at the end of March 1920. Bulgakov was then hired in April 1920 as head of the literary section of the Department of Arts at the Vladikavkaz People's Education Office. The department was headed by the Petersburg writer Yury Slyozkin. Mikhail organized literary evenings for soldiers and citizens, lectured on literature, music, and theater, and taught at a drama studio.

But soon he got into difficulties, and by October 1920 both Bulgakov and Slyozkin were expelled from the Department of Arts.

During this period Bulgakov took his first steps as a playwright, writing several plays which were staged by the local drama theater and studios. They included a one-act humoresque entitled *Samooborona* (Self-defense), and a four-act drama called *Brat'ia Turbiny* (The brothers Turbin). As he described the premiere of *The Brothers Turbin* on 6 June 1920, Mikhail expressed his frustration and disappointment:

> My life is suffering. . . . You cannot imagine how sad I was because my play was performed in a god-forsaken place. . . . The audience shouted "Author!" and applauded. . . . When I was called out after the second act, I appeared on stage with mixed feelings. I looked at the madeup faces of the actors and at the applauding theater audience. And I thought, "this is the fulfillment of my dream . . . but how ugly it is: instead of a Moscow stage, a provincial one, instead of the drama about Alyosha Turbin, which I cherished, a hastily done immature work. Fate is a scoffer."[6]

At the same time Mikhail wrote comic sketches, some of which were published. For example, "Dan' voskhishcheniia" (A tribute of admiration), one of his first stories dealing with the Civil War, was published in the respectable Vladikavkaz newspaper *Kavkazskaia gazeta* (Caucasus gazette) on 5 February 1920. After the establishment of Soviet power in Vladikavkaz a few months later, Bulgakov's witty sketches were published in a new newspaper, *Kommunist* (Communist). In his spare time he worked on his cherished project—a novel.

Mikhail's wife Tatyana joined him in Vladikavkaz in the summer of 1920. To help him make a living, she acted as an extra in the theater where his plays were performed. But life in Vladikavkaz was difficult: Mikhail had no income other than sporadic small payments for his occasional writings. On 26 May 1921, he went to Tiflis, the capital of Georgia, at the urging of the editor N. Pokrovsky, who, however, had already left for abroad when Mikhail arrived in Tiflis.

In Tiflis, Mikhail's life was even more difficult, but he continued to write, reworking *The Brothers Turbin* "into a big drama" as he put it. At the end of July 1921 Mikhail and Tatyana went to Batum, a beautiful resort and important harbor on the Black Sea. Mikhail assumed that if his brothers Nikolay and Ivan were still alive, they might be abroad, evacuated with the Volunteer Army. Mikhail himself may have also considered going abroad, but then he decided to go to Moscow by way of Kiev, where he visited his mother and two sisters. Mikhail did not know then that this was the last time he would see his mother, who died of typhus on 1 February 1922. Fortunately, shortly before her death she had happy news: the first letter from her son Nikolay in Zagreb.

At the end of September 1921, after a difficult journey in an overcrowded train, Mikhail arrived in Moscow. In his autobiography he wrote: "For a long time life in Moscow was a torment; to keep myself alive I worked as a newspaper reporter and essayist, and began to hate these professions so devoid of any distinction. At the same time I began to hate the editors. I hate them now, and I will hate them to the end of my life."[7] And indeed Bulgakov was doomed to struggle against editors and censors until the end of his days.

In Moscow: Earlier Period (1921–25)

His arrival in Moscow marks an important turning point in Bulgakov's life: literature became thereafter his only concern. After a short period of lodging in a student dormitory with a friend, Mikhail and Tatyana moved into a shabby room of the overcrowded "nightmarish" apartment 50 at 10 Bolshaya Sadovaya Street, which would figure in several of Bulgakov's stories.

Mikhail accepted any work he could find, sometimes working simultaneously on several assignments. On 1 October 1921 he found a position as a secretary of LITO—the Literary Section of the Political Education Administration. Unfortunately, two months later this section was closed, and Bulgakov had to depend on his work at the *Torgovo-promyshlennyi vestnik* (Trade industrial herald). But this weekly paper was also closed at the beginning of January 1922. Only in March did Mikhail find a job on a new daily paper *Rabochii* (Worker).

The best description of Mikhail and Tatyana's life is given in a letter of 17 November 1921 from Mikhail to his mother: "Not only do I have to work, but I must work furiously. From morning to late at night, and everyday. . . ." Life in Moscow was "a fierce competition, a continuous race, display of initiative, and so on. It is impossible to avoid such a life, otherwise one would perish. I don't want to be among those who perish."[8]

Beginning in the spring of 1922 Mikhail wrote feuilletons for the Berlin-based Russian-language newspaper *Nakanune* (On the eve) and its "Literary Supplement," edited by Alexey Tolstoy, and soon became one of its most popular contributors. *Nakanune* was created in Berlin by a group of Russian emigrés who had begun to reconsider their opposition to the Soviet regime. Hoping that with the proclamation of the New Economic Policy the Soviet system would be liberalized, they restored contacts with the Soviet Union. The paper had its main editorial board in Berlin and a Moscow office, headed by Mikhail Levidov, journalist and Soviet diplomat, and Emily Mindlin. The Moscow office became a meeting place for a number of writers. Bulgakov's affiliation with *Nakanune* continued until this paper was closed at the end of 1924.

During 1923 Mikhail also published several sketches on children and school problems in the magazine *Golos rabotnika prosveshcheniia* (Voice of an education worker). At the beginning of 1923 he began his affiliation with the literary section of the railroad union paper *Gudok* (Whistle). During the three years of his collaboration with this paper Mikhail published about one hundred humorous sketches in it. He considered this work tedious and unworthy, and seldom signed his sketches with his full name, using various pen names instead. He distinguished between this work and his *Nakanune* feuilletons as well as the stories he hoped to publish separately.

Indeed, he published the stories "Diavoliada" ("Diaboliad") and "Khanskii ogon' " (Khan's fire) in 1924. He also printed two fragments of his semi-autobiographical work "Notes on the Cuffs" in serious publications in 1923. Bulgakov's dream was to publish his *Notes on the Cuffs* in full, but he encountered many obstacles. In his autobiographical sketch of 1924 Bulgakov spoke of his frustrated hopes of ever seeing his first book in print: "No longer by the light of a candle, but by that of a dim electric bulb did I write the book *Notes on the Cuffs*. The Berlin publishing house *Nakanune* bought this book from me and promised to publish it in May 1923. But it was never published. At first, I worried a great deal about it, but later I became indifferent."[9]

The year 1924 brought changes in Mikhail's private life: after eleven years he and Tatyana separated, and he married Liubov' Evgenievna Belozerskaya. After his second marriage Mikhail left Bolshaya Sadovaya Street, and rented a room in a small house on Obukhov (now Chistyi) Lane, where they lived about two years.

The play *The Days of Turbins,* and the stories "Rokovye iaitsa" ("The Fatal Eggs") and *Sobach'e Serdtse (Heart of a Dog)* were written in this room. This room also saw the beginning of Mikhail's long friendship with Nikolay Lyamin and his wife, the painter Natalie Ushakova, and with Pavel Popov, the philosopher and literary historian, and his wife Anna Tolstaya, granddaughter of Leo Tolstoy.

In the fall of 1924 Bulgakov completed his novel *Belaia gvardiia (The White Guard)* and the satirical story "The Fatal Eggs"; the story was published in the magazine *Nedra* (Depths) in February 1925, but the novel had a difficult fate. First it began serial publication in a journal that was shut down; then a contract for separate publication was canceled a few days after it was issued.

At this time Bulgakov met many people from Moscow literary circles: the editor of *Nedra,* Nikolay Angarsky, his assistant Peter Zaytsev, the writers Vikenty Veresaev and Andrey Bely, and others. Mikhail's work on *Gudok* gave him a good opportunity to meet frequently with such writers as Yury Olesha, Ilya Ilf, and Valentin Kataev and his younger brother Evgeny Petrov.

The years 1925 and 1926 were the best in Bulgakov's publishing career. In the middle of 1925 the *Nedra* publishing house issued the first collection of Bulgakov's short stories. Some stories were published in newspapers, and two parts of *The White Guard* appeared in the magazine *Rossiia* (Russia). But *Heart of a Dog* was rejected for publication.

In 1926 a small collection of eight humorous stories—*Rasskazy* (Stories)—appeared in Leningrad, and another collection entitled *Traktat o zhilishche* (A Treatise on Housing) in Moscow and Leningrad. All of the stories had been published previously in *Nakanune.*

Rise of a Playwright (1925–29)

After *The White Guard* failed to appear in full, Bulgakov decided to write a play based on the same material with encouragement from Boris Vershilov, a Moscow Art Theater producer. On 29 January 1926 Bulgakov read his play at the Art Theater, and rehearsals started. Konstantine Stanislavsky, its famous director, required several changes, including a revision of the final scene for ideological reasons. [10]

It took from the fall of 1925 to the fall of 1926 to give the play a form judged acceptable for production, especially since the Main

Repertory Committee required even further changes. Bulgakov was reluctant to make many changes, and tried hard to retain some episodes that were precious to him. But Stanislavsky knew that even the original title in and of itself would cause the play to be banned, so it was renamed *The Days of the Turbins*. When the last public dress rehearsal was held, on 2 October 1926, A. Orlinsky, a member of the Main Repertory Committee, opposed the performance of the play. At a public discussion at the Communist Academy that evening on "The Theater Policy of the Soviet Power," Orlinsky and some other critics attacked Bulgakov so severely that, three days later, the Art Theater administration did not even dare invite him to the premiere. Shortly thereafter Bulgakov and his play became the target of a violent slander campaign launched in the press by Orlinsky and his allies, during which Orlinsky accused Bulgakov of being one of the "new ideological agents" of the bourgeoisie in the theater, and urged the rejection of "Bulgakovism."[11]

Paradoxically, the most virulent criticism came from Anatoly Lunacharsky, people's commissar for education, who had sanctioned the premiere of the play. He accused Bulgakov of approaching the Revolution "in a Philistine manner" without any "class basis." In his mockery Lunacharsky went so far as to call Colonel Alexey Turbin, the play's protagonist, "a professional killer."[12] In short, as soon as White Guard officers appeared on stage as sympathetic human beings, all the critics who dominated the Soviet press and followed the official line branded Bulgakov a supporter of the "White Guardists," a dangerous political accusation at that time.

Bulgakov responded to this political criticism only once, on 7 February 1927, during a public discussion at the Meyerhold Theater. Referring to Orlinsky, who had spoken before him, Bulgakov said that Orlinsky was maliciously misinterpreting *The Days of the Turbins* in his numerous articles.[13] Pavel Markov, the head of the Art Theater Literary Section, defended Bulgakov's play at the same discussion, and remarked that the last act, which had been reworked several times at the demand of the Repertory Committee, "was written by at least fifteen people." Much later, in 1962, Markov recalled this entire episode: "Now it is almost impossible to imagine the belligerent heated atmosphere created by this production of the Art Theater, a production that became almost legendary in the history of the Soviet theater."[14] But Bulgakov had to live in the midst of that abusive campaign. He preserved 301 newspaper reviews in an album:

of those only three were laudatory. In the meantime, however, theatergoers flocked enthusiastically to the ticket windows. The performances were always sold out, and the play's success was enormous.

The years 1926–28 marked the high point of Bulgakov's career as a playwright. On 28 October 1926, three weeks after the brilliant premiere of *The Days of the Turbins,* his comedy *Zoikina Kvartira (Zoyka's Apartment)* premiered at the Vakhtangov Theater. It had been written at the suggestion of Alexey Popov, the producer of the Third Studio of the Moscow Art Theater (later renamed the Vakhtangov Theater). Bulgakov had signed a contract with this theater for it on 1 January 1926. This satirical play dealing with actual problems of life during the NEP period and performed by outstanding actors enjoyed a lasting popular success, but again prompted hostile reviews from such critics as Orlinsky. The orthodox critics denounced the play as philistine and counterrevolutionary.[15] *Zoyka's Apartment,* however, survived the hostile criticism almost three seasons and was performed nearly two hundred times.

Since early 1927 Bulgakov had been working on a satirical comedy, *Bagrovyi ostrov (The Crimson Island),* which the Kamerny Theater accepted for production on 14 March. Simultaneously Bulgakov worked on another play—now known as *Beg (Flight)*—and in April 1927 signed a contract with the Moscow Art Theater for its production.

Soon Bulgakov and his wife rented an apartment at 35a Bolshaya Pirogovskaya Street, where Mikhail lived until February 1934. In the summer of 1927 the couple spent their vacation in the Crimea. In the same year a German translation of *The White Guard* appeared.

In the fall of 1927 the Art Theater was requested to cancel the performances of *The Turbins.* Stanislavsky protested to Lunacharsky that this would ruin the entire plan of the Theater for the coming theatrical season, and Lunacharsky allowed performances of *The Turbins* to continue "at least for the current season."

On 1 March 1928 Bulgakov signed a contract with the Art Theater for his play *Flight,* and on 16 March delivered the text. But on 18 May the play was banned by the Main Repertory Committee. The members of the Committee, who had previously attacked *The Turbins,* criticized *Flight* because, as their resolution said, it depicted "the agony of great heroes, legendary generals," and was a play in which "even Wrangel was characterized by the author as 'brave and noble.' "[16]

Nevertheless, the Art Theater continued its efforts to stage the play, and organized a discussion of it on 9 October 1928. The producer informed the audience that the playwright would make several changes in it, and Vladimir Nemirovich-Danchenko and Maxim Gorky defended it vigorously.[17] The Repertory Committee disregarded the favorable opinion of these professionals in deciding to ban it. Despite some further efforts to save it, Bulgakov's dream of seeing *Flight* on stage with the same actors who created *The Turbins* was not fulfilled during his lifetime.

In the meantime the Kamerny Theater premiered *The Crimson Island* on 11 December 1928, and a third Bulgakov play appeared on the programs of Moscow theaters that winter. Performed as a witty theatrical show with dance and music, in which the author parodied theater censorship and the simplistic revolutionary pieces acceptable to the Repertory Committee, the play not only attracted a large audience but also immediately prompted numerous negative press reviews. One long article in *Zhizn' iskusstva* (life of art) labeled the playwright a "frustrated philistine" and his play a "mockery of the entire Soviet theater system" that presented the censors—"those responsible Soviet functionaries as idiots."[18] But the fate of *The Crimson Island* was decided by Stalin himself. Vladimir Bill-Belotserkovsky, a former sailor, author of a revolutionary play, and one of Bulgakov's most hostile opponents, made repeated requests for the suppression of *The Turbins*. On 2 February 1929 Stalin responded to him. Although Stalin accepted *The Turbins,* which he saw as a manifestation of the overpowering force of Bolshevism, he castigated *Flight* as an attempt to justify "White guardism," which, he said, was an anti-Soviet phenomenon. Stalin suggested that Bulgakov revise that play to emphasize the positive role of the Bolsheviks. Also, Stalin criticized the Kamerny Theater as "really bourgeois" for having staged *The Crimson Island.*[19]

After such criticism Bulgakov's plays obviously could not be produced. One after another the theaters dropped them from their repertories. In June 1929 *The Turbins* was also prohibited.

In late February 1929 Bulgakov met Elena Sergeevna Shilovskaya; she was married to Evgeny Shilovsky, a well-known Soviet military specialist, and had two sons, Evgeny and Sergey. A lasting relationship developed between them. According to her, when she went to the Caucasus in the summer of 1929, Bulgakov wrote her frequent letters. Upon her return to Moscow, Mikhail gave her a present—a notebook inscribed "To a Secret Friend." In a slightly fictionalized epistolary form he began to tell her, his secret friend, the story of how he had become a playwright. Later Bulgakov would incorporate some passages from it into the *Theatrical Novel*.

As a malicious Soviet journalist noted in September 1929, Bulgakov's plays had vanished from the boards: "Soviet theater does not need such a Bulgakov." Indeed, enormous difficulties befell Bulgakov: he was ousted from the theater world that meant so much to him, publicly defamed, and deprived of any means of support. In a letter to Maxim Gorky of 28 September 1929, Bulgakov pointed out that the banning of all his plays had left him without financial resources: "Briefly, everything that I have written in the past ten years has been destroyed." A few weeks earlier Bulgakov had sent letters to Gorky and to the secretary of the Central Executive Committee, asking their assistance in getting permission to go abroad temporarily with his wife. Both his brothers were living in Paris. His request was never granted.[20]

On 14 October 1929 the Moscow Art Theater asked Bulgakov to return the advance he had received for *Flight*. That same day Bulgakov, exasperated, wrote to a Kiev schoolmate that "everything is completely destroyed."[21]

Such was his state of mind when, in October of 1929, Bulgakov began work on the play *Kabala sviatosh (A Cabal of Hypocrites)*, the story of Molière's last years. In the end the Main Repertory Committee rejected this play as well.

In frustration, seeking some way out, after having written several drafts, Bulgakov sent a letter to the Soviet government at the end of March 1930. The authenticity of the text of the letter, published in Russian and English in the Soviet Union and abroad during the 1960s, is questionable. In her memoirs, Bulgakov's second wife claimed that the six-page copy of a purported Bulgakov letter to the government, which had suddenly begun circulating in Moscow, "had nothing in common with the original letter."[22] The original letter should have been short and contained only the request that the writer be allowed to write; otherwise he would suffer the equivalent of death. The English scholar Lesley Milne, after comparing several drafts and texts of the letter, concluded that the published text was one of many drafts that was never actually mailed. What was mailed was a concise letter answered by a call from Stalin to Bulgakov on 18 April. This call was of major importance, for it again opened the doors of the Moscow Art Theater to Mikhail Bulgakov, this time as part of its staff. Thus began a new period in Bulgakov's life and creative career.

Affiliation with the Moscow Art Theater (1930–36)

The direct result of Stalin's telephone call was Bulgakov's assignment as a literary consultant to the Theater of Working Youth (TRAM). Also, his application of 10 May 1930 to the Art Theater Administration was approved and he began work as an assistant producer. His first work in the Art Theater was a stage adaptation of Gogol's *Mertvye dushi (Dead Souls)*. After more than 300 rehearsals and many radical changes, *Dead Souls* premiered on 28 November 1932, although Bulgakov was disappointed at the treatment of his original text and at the necessity of destroying his original idea.

While he was working on *Dead Souls* in the spring of 1931, Bulgakov turned, for the third time, to a novel he had burned the previous year and began it anew. In March he requested that he be relieved of his position as literary consultant to TRAM. In July Bulgakov was offered a contract by the small Leningrad "Red Theater," and a few days later, by the Vakhtangov Theater to write a play "on the theme of a future war": *Adam and Eve*. However, when he read the play in October, the administrators of the "Red Theater" realized that they could not produce it. The Vakhtangov Theater also rejected the play.

On 26 August 1931 Bulgakov signed a contract with the Leningrad Drama Theater for a stage adaptation of Leo Tolstoy's *War and Peace*, which he finished the following February. On 3 October 1931 Bulgakov received good news: a corrected version of *A Cabal of Hypocrites* had been approved for production everywhere. On 6 October Bulgakov offered it to the Leningrad Drama Theater, but the following March the theater rejected the play and canceled the contract. This time Bulgakov attributed his misfortune to a specific enemy: the revolutionary playwright Vsevolod Vishnevsky, who had attacked Bulgakov in the press.

Despite this disappointment, the year 1932 was a remarkable one, and witnessed several changes in Bulgakov's life. On 15 January

1932 the Art Theater informed him that production of *The Days of the Turbins* would be resumed immediately. As Bulgakov wrote to a friend at the time, "For the author of the play it means that a part of his life was returned to him." In another letter Bulgakov described the evening of the repremiere, 18 February, where in the streets near the Art Theater people begged for spare tickets. Bulgakov remained backstage, as excited as the actors; but shortly before the end of the performance Stanislavsky sent him a messenger, a beautiful lady who asked him not to take curtain calls. And he dared not respond to the ovation of the enthusiastic audience. [23]

In late March 1932 the Art Theater began sporadically to rehearse *Molière;* on 11 July Bulgakov signed a contract for a book on Molière. In the fall, after eight and a half years of marriage, he and Liubov' Evgenievna decided to separate. In September Elena Sergeevna Shilovskaya divorced her husband, and in early October married Bulgakov.

The manuscript of Bulgakov's biographical novel on Molière was delivered on 5 March 1933. On 7 April Bulgakov received a letter from Alexander Tikhonov, an editor of the Biographical Series, requesting that he rewrite it in a conventional way. Tikhonov also found in his book "some allusions" to "Soviet reality," and asked Bulgakov to replace his narrator with the objective view of a "serious Soviet historian." Maxim Gorky, the founder of the series in which it was to appear, did not support Bulgakov this time; he agreed with Tikhonov's negative evaluation, saying that not only should the "jovial" style of Bulgakov's narrator be eliminated, but that the historical material should be given the necessary "social significance." On this occasion Bulgakov decided "not to give battle" and refused to rework his book.

However, Bulgakov had to live, and so on 18 May 1934, he contracted with the Leningrad Music Hall to write "an eccentric, synthetic three-act play," at that time untitled. Apparently, Bulgakov had begun to work on it in 1929; in 1933 it was called *Blazhenstvo* (Bliss). In mid-July, the Bulgakovs made a ten-day trip to Leningrad during which he met and befriended the poet Anna Akhmatova. While still in Leningrad, he resumed work on his novel, which, as he wrote to the author Vikenty Veresaev, had been "destroyed three years ago." The same summer, Bulgakov revised *Flight* at the suggestion of Art Theater producer Ilya Sudakov.

The year 1934 brought some positive changes in the Bulgakovs'
living conditions: in February they moved into a building inhabited
mostly by writers on Nashchokinsky Lane (now Furmanov Street).
In March Bulgakov signed a contract with a Moscow film studio
for a filmscript based on Gogol's *Dead Souls*. After several changes
introduced at the request of the directors of the film studio and the
film committee at the Central Committee of the Party, the script
was approved in 1935, but never produced.

In April 1934 Bulgakov successfully offered *Bliss* to the Moscow
Theater of Satire, though the administration soon asked for several
changes. Along with his creative writing, Bulgakov spent a great
deal of time at the Art Theater, attending the rehearsals of *Molière*.

Although Bulgakov always preserved his usual calm good humor,
the stresses of his life fatigued him. In the spring of 1934 he tried
once more to go abroad for two months with his wife, Elena
Sergeevna. On 17 May Bulgakov submitted the necessary travel
documents and the same evening began to dictate the first chapter
of a projected book on a trip abroad to his wife, but his trip abroad
was suddenly canceled. For the third time Mikhail's dream of seeing
his brothers Nikolay and Ivan in Paris—where Nikolay was a well-
known bacteriologist and Ivan a musician—of viewing Molière's
monument "La Fontaine de Molière" with his own eyes, was dashed.
On 7 June Bulgakov fell ill. Only on 13 July could he go to
Leningrad, where he attended the 500th performance of *The Days
of The Turbins,* presented by the Moscow Art Theater, on 20 July.

In August the Ukraine Film Studio asked Bulgakov to write a
filmscript based on Gogol's comedy *Revizor (The Inspector General),*
in connection with which Bulgakov spent five days in Kiev. His
work on this filmscript was difficult, as usual. In 1935 some episodes
of the film were shot, but they were criticized by the members of
the Central Commission on films, and filming was discontinued in
February 1936.

Bulgakov also continued his creative writing: on 9 October 1934
he signed a new contract with the Theater of Satire for a new version
of *Bliss,* now entitled *Ivan Vasil'evich.* He conceived also a plan for
a new play about Pushkin's last days, and the writer Vikenty Veresaev, author of a book on Pushkin, agreed to collaborate with him.

By the middle of 1934 the Art Theater was working on the play
Molière (a new title for *A Cabal of Hypocrites*), with Stanislavsky
having decided to direct the play himself, assigning Bulgakov as

assistant producer. The rehearsal records show that Stanislavsky disagreed with Bulgakov's concept of *Molière:* the director saw Molière as a successful, energetic playwright at the peak of his career, whereas Bulgakov presented Molière as a brilliant playwright suffering in his creative struggle. The minutes of the rehearsals reflect the tense atmosphere in which the play took final shape. In the end Bulgakov accused Stanislavsky of producing a different play from the one he had submitted, and asked that it be returned to him. At the end of 1935 Stanislavsky turned over responsibility for the production to Nemirovich-Danchenko.

Disagreements between Bulgakov and Veresaev in connection with the writing of the play *Alexander Pushkin* created further psychological burdens. The correspondence between them from May to December 1935 reflects their divergences: Veresaev wanted the play to be truly documentary, while Bulgakov wished to re-create artistically the conditions under which Pushkin's duel and death occurred. Finally Veresaev ended their joint authorship.

To get away temporarily from all his troubles, Bulgakov again requested permission to go abroad for three months; and, as usual, his request was denied.

In December 1935 Bulgakov signed a contract with the "Academia" publishing house for a translation of Molière's *L'Avare (The Miser)*. This translation, completed in early February 1936, was Bulgakov's last tribute to his favorite playwright and his only work on Molière published during his lifetime.[24]

In 1936 Bulgakov endured a series of severe blows. The premiere of *Molière*—on 15 February—was successful, but even before the play opened officially Bulgakov's old foe Osaf Litovsky, who headed the Main Repertory Committee, launched an attack on it in *Sovetskoe iskusstvo* (Soviet art).[25] Litovsky criticized the play as "nothing more than a typical philistine melodrama" and intimated it should never have been staged.

The premiere and ensuing performances were successful with the public but *Pravda* soon accused Bulgakov of falsifying history and neglecting the class struggle at the time of Louis XIV in "this false, worthless play." The next day drama critic Boris Alpers seconded that criticism by *Pravda*.[26]

The Art Theater drew its "conclusions" and barred the play, which, after five years of delay and 290 rehearsals, was performed only seven times. For Bulgakov, it was the second death of *Molière*.

At this stage Bulgakov realized that further affiliation with the Art Theater was pointless, and he began work on a textbook on the history of the Soviet Union with the intention of entering a competition sponsored by the Council of the People's Commissariat for Education and the Central Committee of the Party. However, he abandoned this unlikely task after writing several chapters.[27]

The ban of *Molière* affected other Bulgakov plays: his comedy *Ivan Vasil'evich* was removed from the repertory of the Theater of Satire, one week before the premiere. Since Bulgakov refused to make the changes required by the Vakhtangov Theater in *Alexander Pushkin,* it was also withdrawn. Thus, only two of Bulgakov's plays were still performed: *The Days of the Turbins* and *Dead Souls.*

However, in June Bulgakov was asked by the composer Boris Asafiev and the artistic director of the Bolshoi Opera to write a libretto for the opera *Minin and Pozharsky.* Bulgakov completed the libretto by July 1936, at which point Asafiev began to write the music. After several delays, the opera was finished in December 1938, but it was never produced.

After another unsuccessful attempt at collaboration with the Moscow Art Theater, on 15 September 1936 Bulgakov resigned from it and five weeks later accepted a new position as consultant-librettist at the Bolshoi Opera. He was to write one opera libretto a year, review other libretti, and advise the producers on new performances. As his dream of becoming a successful playwright vanished, he shifted to a new form of creative activity.

Last Years (1936–40)

In the middle of November 1936 Bulgakov began to write a novel based on his theatrical experiences, first called *Notes of A Dead Man,* then later *Theatrical Novel.* By September 1937 Bulgakov put it aside to devote all the time he could spare from his work with the Bolshoi Opera to a novel on the devil, now designated definitely as *The Master and Margarita.* But still continued writing plays: on 3 December 1936 he had signed a contract with the Vakhtangov Theater for a stage adaptation of *Don Quixote.*

At the end of May 1938 Bulgakov finished the sixth version of *The Master and Margarita,* which he dictated to his wife's sister. Bulgakov's letters to his vacationing wife during this time provide valuable information on the book, which he was unshakably determined to complete. On 15 June 1938 Bulgakov wrote his wife that she would probably have to put the book away somewhere. He had already rendered judgment on his novel, he said, adding, "but no one knows whether he will ever know the verdict of readers."[28] The typing was finished on 24 June, and the next day Bulgakov joined his wife and stepson in Lebedyan', where he spent a month working on *Don Quixote*. Subsequently Bulgakov gave readings of the novel to friends.[29]

In the meantime, Bulgakov was unsuccessful in his work as a librettist at the Opera, for here too he objected to reworking his libretti in accordance with the views of the authorities. Thus, he completed the libretto for *Peter the Great* by September 1937, but was asked to revise it. He finished a libretto known as *The Black Sea* in 1937, but the Bolshoi abandoned the idea of such an opera, apparently under the pressures created by *Pravda*'s articles of January and February 1936 against Dmitry Shostakovich and "bourgeois ideology" in the Soviet arts. Bulgakov's last libretto, *Rachel*, based on a story by Guy de Maupassant and completed in early 1939, encountered the same fate.

On the advice of friends from the Art Theater, Bulgakov made one more attempt to reenter the theatrical world. Although he rejected their suggestion that he write a play about Stalin's early revolutionary activities, he responded to a second proposal in 1939 and undertook *Pastyr'* (A Pastor), later known as *Batum*, for the Art Theater while simultaneously working on *The Master and Margarita*. On 14 May 1939 he finished the epilogue of the novel, which he read to his friends the same evening.

On 24 July 1939, Bulgakov submitted *Batum* to the director of the Art Theater; it was accepted for production and scheduled for 21 December 1939. Although Bulgakov had his doubts about it, on 14 August he left for Batum with his wife and a team from the Art Theater to prepare the production at the site of the action. A few hours after their departure, a telegram arrived ordering the team to return to Moscow because the play had been banned. The Bulgakovs left the train in Tula, rented a car, and by evening returned home. Bulgakov was very ill, with sharp pains in his eyes for the first time.

On 10 September Bulgakov took a leave from the Bolshoi and went to Leningrad with his wife, where a doctor diagnosed his disease as hypertonic nephrosclerosis, the illness of which his father had died. Later, Moscow physicians confirmed the diagnosis, but Bulgakov refused to go to the hospital because he wanted to work on the corrections to *The Master and Margarita.*

By early October he could no longer read. On 10 October he dictated his will to a lawyer. On 16 November his wife signed a contract for him with a Leningrad theater for a production of *Don Quixote.*

At the end of November 1939 the Bulgakovs went to a convalescent home near Moscow, but shortly returned to the capital. Bulgakov was aware that his illness was terminal: on 28 December he wrote to a Kiev schoolfriend that he was plagued by the thought that he had "returned to die."

During this period Alexander Fadeev, secretary of the Union of the Soviet Writers, visited the Bulgakovs and perhaps realized what a wrong had been done to this talented writer, whom he had never tried to help. Now Bulgakov was beyond help: he knew, as he said to his neighbor, that he was dying, adding: "It must be—that is normal. No comments."[30]

On 25 January 1940, apparently for the last time, Bulgakov went out for a short walk; three days earlier his wife had signed a contract for him with the Art Theater for the production of *Alexander Pushkin.* Though his health was steadily deteriorating, in 1940 he made several changes in the typescript of *The Master and Margarita.* According to his wife, in the middle of February, when she began to read him a passage about Berlioz's funeral, Bulgakov said: "Well, it is enough, I think."[31] And indeed the corrections his wife inserted at his dictation stop at that place.

Numerous friends were at Bulgakov's bedside during his last days, besides his wife, his youngest sister, and other family members. Mikhail Bulgakov died in his sleep on 10 March, at 4:40 P.M., at the age of forty-nine.

On 12 March his coffin was borne past the Art Theater and to the Bolshoi Opera, where the actors came out to take leave of their colleague. The body was cremated and interred at Novodevich'e cemetery in Moscow. Vasily Sakhnovsky, producer and artistic director of the Moscow Art Theater, spoke at a brief ceremony at the crematorium. Bulgakov's two final plays—*Don Quixote* and *Pushkin* (or *Last Days*), both ending with the death of the protagonist— were premiered posthumously: *Don Quixote* on 13 March 1941, at the Pushkin State Academic Theater in Leningrad, and on 8 April at the Vakhtangov Theater in Moscow. *Last Days,* whose forthcoming production Sakhnovsky mentioned in his speech, premiered at the Art Theater on 10 April 1943.

In 1952, at the initiative of Bulgakov's widow, a large black granite stone was placed on Mikhail's grave, a stone brought from the Crimea some 100 years earlier by the writer Sergey Aksakov for Gogol's grave. When Gogol's remains were transferred from the Danilov Monastery to the Novodevich'e cemetery, a new monument was erected. The placing of this stone on Bulgakov's grave affirmed symbolically the affinity between Bulgakov and Gogol. In July 1970 Elena Sergeevna Bulgakova was buried beside him.

Chapter Two
Semi-autobiographical Works

Several of Bulgakov's earlier stories depict, in fictionalized form, episodes drawn from his own life. These works are characterized by a slight shifting and merging of real events, time, and places, and the use of a first-person narrator who frequently represents a simplified and ironically portrayed image of the writer's alter ego. Indeed, special devices designed to separate Bulgakov as author from his narrators do not always veil the basic parallelism between them. Although it would be an exaggeration to equate a work of art with an objectively told life story, most of Bulgakov's biographers include some of his stories, especially *A Country Doctor's Notebook*, in their material. Therefore, when comparing the real facts of Bulgakov's life, as known from original documents and other reliable sources, with episodes depicted in his stories, we should remember that, though semi-autobiographical, they are still works of the writer's creative imagination. Their importance lies mainly in their evocative powers: they help to re-create the historical and social background as well as the psychological and emotional climate in which their author lived.

A Country Doctor's Notebook

The work most closely associated with Bulgakov's first position in life—his assignment to a small hospital in Nikolskoe—is *Zapiski iunogo vracha (A Country Doctor's Notebook)*. By the time he re-created the real events of the time in his fiction, the fears and difficulties of that distant period seemed to him almost comic.

The *Notebook* consists of a series of episodes covering one-and-a-half years in the life of a young physician just out of medical school. Though the narrator's situation generally parallels Bulgakov's own experience, there are still some very important differences.

Bulgakov was twenty-five years old when he arrived in Nikolskoe, while his narrator is only twenty-three. At this age, such a difference can be substantial. A major concern of the narrator was that of concealing his extreme youth as well as his complete lack of medical experience. The second important difference was Bulgakov's marriage: his wife Tatyana helped him in his difficult task at the country hospital. The narrator of the *Notebook* is a naive, lonely bachelor who has no confidant and so frequently talks to himself about medical problems. Though Bulgakov changed some important facts and names in *Notebook* he used exact dates (16 and 17 September) and actual circumstances in describing the doctor's arrival in the provincial town of Grachovka and at the hospital in the village of Muryevo.

The doctor's first impressions of provincial reality were rather gloomy. Accustomed to watching operations performed by a group of professors in a vast gleaming hall, he suddenly found himself in a world of muddy roads, cold rains, infinite gray fields, and poor peasant huts. However, unexpectedly, despite the lack of electricity and transportation facilities, the doctor found the hospital well equipped. Thanks to his able predecessor, the medical library was well stocked with Russian and German medical texts, and the hospital had an excellent set of surgical instruments, many of them unfamiliar to the doctor.

The hospital staff—medical assistant Demyan Lukich, who excelled in the art of extracting teeth; two midwives, Anna Nikolaevna and Pelageya Ivanovna; their two helpers; and the watchman—welcomed their young chief. But their talk about the craft of his legendary predecessor made the doctor wonder whether he could deal with every eventuality.

In the midst of his hesitations, the doctor was confronted with harsh reality: amputating the leg of an extremely beautiful young girl. At first his hopeless situation filled the inexperienced young man with despair, but then he gathered his courage and performed his first operation successfully. Two-and-a-half months later the doctor received a long linen towel embroidered with a red rooster from the girl whose life he had saved. [1]

Even more complex cases required the doctor's devotion and growing professional skill. The November "Note" recorded a difficult case of diphtherial croup, from which an angelic three-year-old girl was suffocating. She could only be saved by a tracheotomy, which the doctor had never even observed. But the operation was miraculously successful, and the doctor's patients increased to 110 a day.

Unfortunately, miracles did not occur every day. Thus, the doctor was too late to save the life of a young bride, victim of an absurd accident. He also failed to save a baby who died during a difficult delivery, when the doctor broke its lifeless arm. The doctor waged a constant battle against death: "It began every morning by the pale light reflected from the snow, and ended by the yellow twinkling of a kerosene lamp." And he did not always win the battle: "I felt the usual stab of cold in the stomach that I always feel when I face death. I hate it."[2]

The idealistic doctor was always available to help anyone in need. Once, exhausted by a night journey in a blizzard, almost attacked by hungry wolves, the doctor had a moment of doubt: "I wouldn't go again even if you paid me in gold. . . ." His second inner voice immediately objected: "You will go, yes, you will go. . . ." And even the clock seconded this by ticking: "You will go, go, go. . . ."[3]

On 17 December 1917 his staff celebrated the doctor's birthday and told him all kinds of "anecdotes," such as the one about the peasant who put mustard plasters on his sheepskin coat instead of on his body. And he reaffirmed his loyalty to his vocation: "No, I will fight it . . . I will."[4] He was no longer alone: he had with him his "warrior band"—his assistant and two midwives. Even in his dreams at night he saw them following him, moving forward and fighting for life.

Despite the seriousness of many situations he described, the doctor always found a comic aspect to his work. Thus at the end of his first year, he calculated he had treated 15,613 patients. Of 200 in-patients, only six had died. That impressive record caused the doctor to conclude that he had nothing more to fear. But the very next day shattered his self-assurance: he did not recognize an abscess on a baby boy's eyelid and thought that the eye was missing. Fortunately, the boy's mother prevented him from operating, and a week later brought him the healthy boy with two normal eyes. Then the doctor realized that he would always have something new to learn.

Of Bulgakov's stories—"Zvezdnaia syp' " ("Starry Rash") and "Morfii" ("Morphine") differ significantly from the *Notebook,* though they were also narrated by the same doctor. Bulgakov excluded "Starry Rash" from *A Country Doctor's Notebook* because of its specialized content. It lacks the soft humor of the other stories, but it describes the same snow-covered hospital with its four-man team and contains an important page on the doctor's experience in the country.[5]

Six months after his arrival, the doctor encountered a case of syphilis for the first time. But his peasant patient did not trust him, accepted some mercury ointment disdainfully, and never came back to the hospital.

Soon other cases of this disease appeared, one even involving a two-year-old boy. The doctor decided to fight the disease by establishing special wards for syphilitics, then devoting some years of his later life to the treatment of venereal disease. This story parallels some facts of Bulgakov's real life.

"Morphine,"[6] written and published in 1927, stands apart, and was not included by Bulgakov in the *Notebook* either. It not only lacks Bulgakov's usual humor, but also presents a gloomy view of man's capacity for self-destruction.

"Morphine" consists of two different stories—that of the narrator, a young doctor from a provincial hospital, and the diary of his friend who succeeded him at the country hospital and became a drug addict. The first part continues the story of the narrator of *A Country Doctor's Notebook,* whose name is given here as Vladimir Mikhailovich Bomgard, and whose story coincides partly with Bulgakov's life.

After a year and a half in a small country hospital, remote from civilization, Bomgard was transferred in the fall of 1917 to a larger town. He now headed the children's section of a large, well-equipped hospital and was no longer responsible "for everything that happened in the world," because now his duties were shared by four other doctors.

The description of the hospital and the provincial town, which struck Bomgard as the height of civilization, and his happiness at being freed from his heavy country burden parallel Bulgakov's own feelings during his life in Vyazma from September 1917 to February 1918.

The episode from the life of Sergei Poliakov, Bomgard's former university friend and his successor at the country hospital, has some affinities with an actual episode in Bulgakov's own life, when he almost became addicted to morphine.

In masterly artistic form "Morphine" presents Bulgakov's real-life experience split between two protagonists: Dr. Bomgard, whose image reflected the external conditions of Bulgakov's life in Vyazma; and Dr. Poliakov, whose gloomy last days reflected a dramatic episode in Bulgakov's medical practice. In "Morphine" Bulgakov carried the danger of drug addiction to its logical end, an end which he himself avoided. But Dr. Poliakov went through a hell of hallucinations, split personality, and worsening physical deterioration. Finally, instead of returning to the Moscow psychiatric clinic, which he had once left against the doctor's advice, Poliakov preferred suicide to endless torment.

Critics praised the Notes of the young doctor highly when the six stories appeared in a volume of Bulgakov's selected prose in 1966—twenty years after Bulgakov's death.[7]

"The Extraordinary Adventures of a Doctor"

"Neobyknovennye prikliucheniia doktora" (The extraordinary adventures of a doctor), published in 1922, was one of the first works Bulgakov placed in a Moscow paper. Though the protagonist is a young doctor, the subject of his notes was not his medical practice, but rather troublesome external conditions upon which his fate and acts depended. His notes are preceded by a short preface which sets the ironic-comic tone of the whole story. The author of the preface tells of how he received the manuscript of a friend, a certain Doctor N., who vanished after a mysterious incident in the Caucasus while serving as a field doctor with General Denikin's forces.[8]

Although he did not find the doctor's notes interesting and was barely able to decipher his "abominable" handwriting, he published them anyway, dividing them into short chapters and giving some of them funny titles. The fate of Dr. N. is not known for certain: one version has it that he was killed; another that he drowned during the embarkation of the White Army in Novorossiisk; and a third that Dr. N. was living in Buenos Aires. The author was inclined to accept this third version, and assured his readers that he would send royalties to Dr. N. in Buenos Aires as soon as he received confirmation that he was actually there. Thus this brief preface presents Dr. N. as a naive and humorous figure.

The lighthearted narrative, however, conceals a dramatic story of an apparently apolitical young intellectual, who dreamed of writing a thesis on bacteriology but instead became involved in a massive struggle between opposing forces and several times barely escaped death. The setting is obviously Kiev. In short paragraphs, using simple language, Dr. N. fixed in his notebook events occurring between December 1918 and February 1920.

Bulgakov possessed an astonishing faculty for transforming harsh reality into an almost jovial, absurd anecdote. Paradoxically, Dr. N.'s fragmentary notes encode Bulgakov's impressions of a rather dramatic but less known period of his life, when he served as a field doctor with a Cossack White Army unit. The battles between the Cossacks and the Chechens in Khankal gorge and at Chechen-Aul, presented by Dr. N. as an almost surrealistically devilish nightmare, actually occurred in the Caucasus. Even Uzun-Khadzha, mentioned by Dr. N. as some mysterious spirit of vengeance, was a real person, the leader of the Chechens.[9] Dr. N.'s decision to leave the army has parallels with Bulgakov's withdrawal from his medical service in the White Guard.

Notes on the Cuffs and "Bohème"

Zapiski na manzhetakh (Notes on the cuffs), written in 1922–23 on the basis of Bulgakov's impressions of Vladikavkaz, Tiflis (Tbilisi), and Batum, as well as his arrival in Moscow in 1921, has never been published in full. What has appeared in various periodicals and almanacs are fragments from a highly stylized semi-autobiographical work.[10] Some fragments supplement one another; a few passages are repetitive, but each text contains new details of the same event or a slightly different version. Harsh reality is presented with Bulgakov's usual irony and satirical, sometimes grotesque, touch.

Like "Neobyknovennye prikliucheniia doktora," "Bohème" and *Notes on the Cuffs* help to establish some peripeteia of Bulgakov's life from 1919 to 1921. Along with the feuilletons *Forty Times Forty* and *Moscow in the Twenties, Notes on the Cuffs* contains an artistic transformation of the author's struggle for survival under unusual conditions in a troubled period.

The genre of this fragmentary work is identified by its title: short notes scribbled on cuffs, recollections of a difficult period. Bulgakov said of his work later: "A novelette? No, it was not a novelette, but something like a memoir."[11] *Notes* resembles a diary with entries made in haste, sometimes even in delirium, describing the misadventures, failures, and sufferings of the narrator.

The published text consists of two fragmentary parts. Part 1, set in the Caucasus, opens with the sudden departure of the editor of the newspaper *Russkoe slovo* (Russian word) to Rome, where he still had some money in the Credito Italiano Bank, at the news of the Bolshevik approach to the town. The narrator, addressed by his friends as Mishenka (a diminutive form of Bulgakov's first name Mikhail), wanted to find out what catastrophe had prompted the editor's hasty departure, but he suddenly fell ill.

Unfortunately, he was a victim of typhus, a disease that plagued Russia during the Civil War. The narrator struggled with high fever and delirium. At one point he declared that he wanted to escape and go to Paris: "I will write a novel there, and then I will go to a secluded monastery."[12] When his friends would not immediately let him go to Paris, the patient demanded his gun. This fragment vividly depicts the state of mind of a person vacillating between moments of light and darkness.

Later, the recovering narrator discussed with his friend, the writer Yury Slyozkin—he retained his real name—the eternal problem of "what to do?" in order to survive starvation. Slyozkin's idea of starting a *podotdel iskusstv* ("Subsection of the Arts"), re-creates in a satirical way Bulgakov's activities at the Department of Arts at the Vladikavkaz Peoples' Education Office. Though the narrator became the head of *Lito,* the part of the "Subsection of the Arts" that embraced literature, theater, painting, and photography, he was supervised by an enigmatic man in military uniform who inspired terror in everyone. Soon the narrator started organizing literary evenings and lectures, just as did Bulgakov during the same period.

Typical of those times of reevaluation or drastic rejection of the cultural past is the tragicomic "Istoriia s velikimi pisateliami" (Story with great writers), describing literary evenings devoted to Chekhov and to Pushkin. Unhappily, the uneducated audience completely misunderstands the narrator's lecture on Pushkin, laughing at the most inappropriate moments. Afterwards a certain "debauchee in poetry"—a revolutionary poet—wrote a libelous attack on the narrator in the local newspaper and "Everything was finished . . . ! The literary evenings were banned."[13]

In fragments published in *Nakanune* and *Vozrozhdenie* (Renaissance) under the title "Kamer-iunker Pushkin" (Gentleman of the Emperor Kammerjunker Pushkin), literary evenings are different but have the same tragic ending. When a progressive revolutionary poet declared that he would devote a special lecture to Pushkin, friends urged the narrator to speak as an opponent. When the speaker, after demolishing Pushkin, proposed to throw him into a furnace, the narrator rose to defend Pushkin, but paid for this by malicious attacks in the local press. The slander campaign resulted in the ejection of the narrator and his friend Yury Slyozkin from the "Subsection of the Arts," and Slyozkin's replacement by the "debauchee in poetry." This fictionalized story presented with bitter humor throws light on the real conditions in which Bulgakov worked in Vladikavkaz.

After his dismissal, the narrator was reduced to selling his hat at the local flea market to buy food. In chapter 12, the narrator tells the humorous story of how he earned 100,000 rubles in 1921 (a not inconsiderable sum even during those inflationary times) by coauthoring a bad play on the lives of the native peoples in only seven days, which enjoyed a resounding success with the local Chechens, Kabardins, and Ingush. This story is an artistic transformation of a real episode involving a play of Bulgakov's. The narrator reveals that with the royalties he hoped to reach Paris. [14]

Finally, Vladikavkaz, that "cursed city at the foot of a mountain," is left behind and, in the spring of 1921, the narrator finds himself on the shores of the Black Sea, in Batum. Unsuccessful in finding employment in the local press or theater, the narrator sold his overcoat at the market and tried to embark on a ship going abroad, but failed. And he decided to go home. The *Nakanune* version adds the words: "To Moscow! To Moscow!" [15]

Analogous experiences became the subject of the short story "Bogema" (Bohème), written in 1924. [16] In the first of its two chapters, the narrator returns to his final few days in Vladikavkaz, when "the redoubtable phantom of starvation" knocked at his door followed by a local lawyer, Genzulaev, who inspired the narrator to write a revolutionary play with him based on the life of the local citizenry. And the play did very well: it was performed three times in a local theater, breaking all attendance records.

Royalties from the play allowed the narrator to attempt leaving Vladikavkaz for Tiflis. But in 1921 one needed special permission before boarding a train, and the narrator's claim that he was going to Tiflis to stage his revolutionary play did not satisfy the pistol-toting young man signing permits at the railroad station, who sent the narrator to the Special Interrogation Section. It took some time for the narrator to talk his way out of the situation.

The second chapter of "Bogema" vividly depicts the chaotic traveling conditions of 1921, when the narrator found a place with a group from a political enlightenment section, but only after promising to collaborate in their newspaper by writing feuilletons.

Part 2 of *Notes on the Cuffs* is set in Moscow, with a description of the narrator's arrival at night and a humorous account of his hunt for a job. Soon he was appointed secretary of the Moscow *Lito* ("Literary Section"), housed in a bare room where two persons clad in rags greeted him in a friendly manner and gave him five pounds of dry peas as a quarter of his ration.

The story of the narrator's activities in the Moscow *Lito* in late 1921 basically coincided with the facts of Bulgakov's biography and provides insight into the unstable conditions of that time of transition. Under the narrator's guidance, *Lito* initiated a fine program, but the struggle with red tape continued: paychecks arrived irregularly, and the employees frequently starved. Finally the order came to liquidate *Lito*. The narrator, its loyal secretary, carried it out.

Feuilletons

Several of Bulgakov's feuilletons from his early Moscow years contain autobiographical elements reminiscent of *Notes on the Cuffs*. Thus in the first chapter of *Forty Times Forty* the narrator recalls his arrival in Moscow in late September 1921. His first impression was the darkness and the mist. There were only three lights at the Briansk railroad station and on the bridge. Nonetheless he was enthusiastic, because "Moscow is our Mother, Moscow is our native city."[17]

The narrator remarked that although "now" (in 1923) poets have begun calling those years the "heroic times," he was no hero. He was rather an alien, caught between two opposing social groups. The proletarians treated him, an intellectual, as a second-rate "bourgeois" and tried to have him evicted from his room, while the "bourgeois" rejected him "at the first sight of his clothes," believing him to be a proletarian. He did not perish only because he had "developed an unheard-of monstrous energy."

None of Bulgakov's letters to his relatives reveals so accurately and realistically his hopeless situation in 1921–22 and his desperate struggle for survival as the slightly ironic lines of that feuilleton written for Russian emigrés in Berlin.

The introduction to the cycle of feuilletons *Moscow in the Twenties* emphasized the narrator's close familiarity with reality: "It was not from afar that I studied Moscow in the years 1921–24. Oh no, I lived in it, I tramped through it from one end to the other. I went up to almost every sixth floor on which institutions were located and, since there was not a single sixth floor without an institution, all those floors were quite familiar to me."[18]

The acute housing shortage is a recurrent theme in the *Nakanune* feuilletons, which described the noise, drunken quarrels, and late-night accordion playing that turned life into a nightmare. For Bulgakov, this nightmare was embodied in "the accursed image of Vasily Ivanovich," the apartment manager, whose violence, vulgarity, and constant threats to evict him, a "bourgeois," poisoned Bulgakov's life. The torment of a communal apartment found its most poignant expression in "Samogonnoe ozero" (Moonshine lake), in which the reader learns that by "that time" (the spring of 1923) the narrator and his wife have been living in this apartment for a year and a half, a fact which coincides with Bulgakov's life. The narrator of the story records that when he and his wife returned from Easter Matins, they encountered noise and drunken shouting which continued all day long that Easter Sunday.

Other autobiographical elements occur in "Putevye zametki" (Travel notes) and "Kiev-gorod" (The city of Kiev). In this stylized reportage Bulgakov described a trip from Moscow to Kiev in April 1923 with a feeling of relief and admiration. It was difficult to believe that life was now becoming more normal: one could now even have meals in the dining car. Bulgakov rejoiced to see his beloved Kiev again, "the most beautiful city in Russia."[19]

Traces of the Civil War were still visible everywhere, but Bulgakov made "an excursion into the Realm of History" and recalled with delight the peaceful Kiev of "legendary times," when his "carefree young generation" was growing up. This passage is imbued by nostalgia for the beauty of sunsets on the Dnepr River and for his happy youth. Bulgakov expressed the hope that perhaps one day someone would write a book about the great battles of Kiev following the revolution of March 1917. He summarizes Kiev's martyrdom with a statement quoted by a number of his biographers: "Now one can say: according to the Kievans' record, they had eighteen upheavals. Some war memorists count twelve; I can say precisely that there were fourteen upheavals, ten of which I experienced personally."[20]

Theatrical Novel

At the end of his life Bulgakov once more reviewed his past experience in fictionalized form by writing *Teatral'nyi roman (Theatrical Novel)*, a book about the theater and the playwright's profound love for theatrical art. Bulgakov began work on it in November 1936,[21] after the difficulties which caused him to abandon the theater.

Early drafts of a work on the theater, dated September 1929, were contained in a manuscript addressed "To a Secret Friend," with the proposed titles: "Followers of Dionysus," "Altar of Dionysus," "Scenes," or "Tragedy Flaunts a Tawdry Robe." But "To a Secret Friend" is much more personal in style, and lacks the frequently ironic, jocular overtones of *Theatrical Novel*. Moreover, it contains several of the author's direct reminiscences, as, for example the horrifying scene of the beating of a Jewish tailor on a troubled winter night in Kiev, and the tragic fate of his younger brother who Bulgakov thought had been killed in the Civil War. Also, its general tone is much gloomier: "Laying my head on the table cloth, I thought of the hopelessness of my situation. Once I had lived a good life, but suddenly everything had vanished, like smoke, and I found myself in Moscow, in a room, alone. . . . An hour passed. The entire house was still silent, and it seemed to me that I was alone in the whole city of Moscow as if incarcerated in a stony pit. . . ."[22]

In addition, "To a Secret Friend" contains valuable material about Bulgakov's first impressions of the office of the newspaper *Gudok,* his method of writing funny sketches for the newspaper, and his attitude toward this type of boring work.

Structurally *Theatrical Novel* is a complex work; various narrative styles and themes are interwoven to create a large background of Moscow theatrical and literary activities against which the tragicomic story of a young playwright named Maksudov unfolds. A curious insight into backstage life is mingled with his naive admiration of the mysterious and esoteric theater world as well as with his romantic hopes of becoming part of that world. The resulting texture is translucent enough to reveal another reality behind the disguised characters and constantly shifting situations. Maksudov's narration is full of allusions to facts and subtle details drawn from Bulgakov's own experience. Scenes of genuine hilarity and humor alternate with lyrical declarations of love for theatrical art and with a deep but concealed frustration.

Theatrical Novel is cast in the form of notes left by someone and published by the author. In a short preface the author ostensibly separates himself from Maksudov and sets the tone of the story that follows. Although the preface to *Theatrical Novel* speaks of notes left by a young suicide, it lacks "Morphine"'s gloomy, desperate touch, which is rare in Bulgakov's works.

The preface to *Theatrical Novel* tells how the author received a manuscript sent to him from Kiev by Sergei Maksudov, who asked that it be published after his suicide. The author fulfilled Maksudov's last wish, but also insisted, as one familiar with the Moscow theatrical world, that Maksudov was never affiliated with any theater, and the whole story was the fruit of his sick imagination. And he downplayed the effect of Maksudov's dramatic suicide, commenting that he had had to correct the punctuation in Maksudov's carelessly written manuscript: "And what can one expect from a man who, two days after he placed the last period in his notes, threw himself headlong from the Chain Bridge [in Kiev]."[23]

Maksudov's notes consist of two parts. Part 1 has fourteen chapters, while part 2 has only two chapters, and the title of the second, "A Successful Marriage," does not reflect its content. This creates the impression of a manuscript suddenly interrupted by Maksudov's suicide. The notes begin with a letter to Maksudov from Ilchin, a producer of the Independent Theater, who had read his novel. In chapter 2–7 Maksudov tells the story of his writing the novel and of its partial publication. Chapters 8–11 are devoted to his work on the stage adaptation of the novel. Chapter 12 contains a humorous description of a reading before the powerful director of the Independent Theater, and Maksudov's refusal to make the major alterations demanded of him.

After three months of loneliness, Maksudov was suddenly summoned to attend rehearsals of his play. However, the actors spent their time doing exercises according to a well-known "system," while the acting director and the producer insisted on further changes, so that the author of the play *Black Snow* lost all hope of ever seeing his work performed. And yet his love for the theater was even more important to him than his play. As Maksudov put it in the last sentence of his notes, he was "Consumed with love for the Independent Theater, pinned to it like a beetle to a cork. . . ."[24]

This apparently simple story about a young playwright's failure is closely connected with two areas of Russian life of the 1920s and 1930s—literature and theater. To be sure, *Theatrical Novel* is a work of art, a timeless drama of an artist struggling for recognition for his work. Still, one who is familiar with Bulgakov's life will find parallels between real events and the imaginary story of Sergei Maksudov.

For instance, in speaking of his past life, Maksudov said that he had lived in several different worlds, and they were identical to Bulgakov's. One world was the university laboratory, of which he remembered only the fume chamber and retorts on the stands, and which he had to leave during the Civil War.

The story of how Maksudov wrote his novel at night, during time free from his tedious work at the *Shipping Herald,* recalls Bulgakov's situation as he was writing *The White Guard.* The second chapter— "The Onset of Neurosis"—contains a beautiful description of the emergence of the author's creative drive, when Maksudov felt an urge to write about a dream of a snowstorm in his native city, of a cozy room with a piano and a shaded lamp, in a reminiscence of Bulgakov's own yearning for his home in Kiev. After several months of intense work Maksudov finished his novel, but no publishing house would accept it. After all his hopes were crushed, Maksudov decided to commit suicide. He stole a gun from a friend, but as he was about to pull the trigger, he suddenly heard a phonograph downstairs playing *Faust,* his favorite opera, and decided to wait for Mephistopheles' aria "For the Last Time." This saved his life: at the last moment a character very much like Mephistopheles appeared. Although he resembled the famous devil, he was in fact Ilya Rudolfi, editor of one of the last privately owned magazines remaining in the Soviet Union, who quickly accepted and published the novel. Rudolfi is reminiscent of a real person, Isai Lezhnev, who serialized two parts of Bulgakov's novel *The White Guard* in *Rossiia.*

Theatrical Novel is a kind of modern roman à clef. Its style and genre are in the vein of 1920s jest-farces, which were popular in Russian theaters, when actors improvised brief comic scenes in their own intimate circles by parodying each other and re-creating humorous episodes. Bulgakov had an extraordinary facility for comic extemporization. The situation of the time, with its complicated conditions for literary creativity and the necessity of adjusting to the requirements of the authorities, provided abundant material for caricature.

By no means are all the numerous heroes of *Theatrical Novel* based on real people, but some are. Thus Maksudov's notes include a satirical description of a party given in honor of the famous writer Izmail Alexandrovich Bondarevsky, who had just returned from Paris. Indeed, the writer Alexey Nikolaevich Tolstoy, editor in chief of the literary supplement of *Nakanune,* returned to Moscow in June 1923 as did three other members of its staff after several years of life abroad. At public meetings Tolstoy spoke about life abroad and read a short story giving a negative picture of the life of Russian emigrés. Alexey Tolstoy's behavior, his pathetic style of speech, and his pretensions at being a "great writer" served Bulgakov as a basis for Izmail Bondarevsky's portrayal. Another writer, Likospastov, Maksudov's "elderly" friend, seems to combine features of two persons—Bulgakov's friend Yuri Slyozkin and his colleague on *Gudok,* Valentin Kataev, who is also mentioned by Maksudov separately as "a young man" who had surprised him "by the way he wrote short stories with such inimitable skill." Both Slyozkin and Kataev portrayed Bulgakov in their stories negatively.[25]

The pages devoted to the "Independent Theater" are full of hints at real people and situations connected with the Moscow Art Theater, including Vladimir Nemirovich-Danchenko, the critic Pavel Markov, and the producer Ilya Sudakov.

Almost everything about theater life had a magical attraction for Maksudov. Most of all he admired the ability of the actors to reincarnate themselves instantaneously in another personage. He praised the wonderful young actor Patrikeev in the role of a "minor official in love with a woman who did not love him"; Patrikeev is easily identified with Mikhail Yanshin, who played Larion in *The Days of the Turbins.* A delighted Maksudov several times attended a play "in which they wore Spanish costumes and where one actor played the servant so comically, and so superbly, that I broke out in a gentle sweat of sheer pleasure."[26] Here he has in mind Nikolay Batalov, who created the brilliant Figaro in Beaumarchais's *Marriage of Figaro,* produced in 1927 by the Art Theater. Maksudov also admired the complete mastery of the powerful director Ivan Vasilievich: watching him offer a bouquet in a rehearsal, Maksudov realized that Ivan Vasilievich was "an actor of genius."[27]

A scene in the office of Filipp Filippovich ("Filya") Tulumbasov, "the most popular man in Moscow," presented so accurate a picture of this "magic" office that Filya's prototype—Fedor ("Fedya") Nikolaevich Mikhalsky, inspector of the Art Theater—referred to Bulgakov's pages instead of describing the office himself in a special chapter of his book on the Moscow Art Theater.[28]

Maksudov's notes abound in comic episodes where Bulgakov's inexhaustible wit found brilliant expression: scenes in the office of Poliksena Toropetskaya, secretary to Aristarkh Platonovich; the signing of a restrictive contract in the luxurious office of the theater's business manager, Gavriil Stepanovich; the admiring of the portrait gallery in the theater hall; and the hilarious scene at the Independent Theater in front of a poster announcing a new repertory for the coming season, where, surprisingly, Maksudov found his name concluding an impressive list of world-famed playwrights from Aeschylus and Sophocles to Schiller and Ostrovsky.

Along with scenes of sparkling humor, Maksudov's notes contain quite bitter statements, especially on the subject of the authorities' forcing the playwright to make alterations to fit their requirements. Indeed, as we know, Bulgakov had to change against his wishes several scenes from his plays at the insistence of Stanislavsky and the members of the Main Repertory Committee. In *Theatrical Novel* the despotic figure of Ivan Vasilievich embodied all the authorities upon whom the fate of the playwright depended. A comic scene in the home of Ivan Vasilievich, who demanded such drastic changes as to destroy Maksudov's play, had its painful origin in Bulgakov's own personal experiences.

In *Theatrical Novel,* comprised of sparkling jest-farces interspersed with serious meditations on theatrical and acting art, the profound drama of the playwright was revealed in one sentence of Maksudov's: "I realized that it is impossible to write plays and not be able to perform them."[29] From this moment he was again plagued with the thought of a second suicide attempt.

Maksudov succumbed to this temptation because he knew that to live he needed the theater just as an addict needs morphine. Chapter 9, entitled "Beginnings," makes it clear that Maksudov started compiling his reminiscences only after he had decided to commit suicide. Recalling the day when he was summoned to the theater to sign the contract for the production of his play, Maksudov wrote: "Soon I will cease to exist, very soon I will be no more! I have made a decision, but it is still rather frightening. . . . But even while dying I will remember that office in which I was received by Gavriil Stepanovich, the theater's business manager."[30]

And in fact Maksudov interrupted his memoirs, wrote a farewell letter to his friend, the prospective publisher of his memoirs, and went to his native Kiev to take his life. Bulgakov needed the theater as much as Maksudov, though he limited himself to an act of moral suicide: withdrawal from the Moscow Art Theater. But then a miracle occurred. Bulgakov the playwright committed symbolic suicide in the person of Maksudov to arise again as a prose writer, for in the fall of 1937 Bulgakov put aside *Theatrical Novel* and turned to *The Master and Margarita,* one of the foremost works of Russian prose in this century.

Until now *Theatrical Novel* has received only limited critical attention.[31] Some critics have praised it as an extremely witty work; others have underestimated its complex meaning and structure; while still others have minimized its bitter and sarcastic essence. Michael Glenny has underlined the sarcastic aspect of the novel: in his introduction to his English translation of *Theatrical Novel* he called *Black Snow* "Bulgakov's revenge on Stanislavsky for the failure of *Molière.*"[32] Although this opinion has some validity, the general theme of the novel is broader and more profound: it is mainly a drama about a man who never achieved recognition and whose dreams of devoting his entire life to the theater were forever frustrated.

Vasily Toporkov, who came to the Art Theater in 1927 and knew Bulgakov well, contributed a valuable opinion in his afterword to the first publication of *Theatrical Novel* in 1965. Toporkov praised the novel, characterizing it as "tragicomic," and adding that with the sharp eye of a satirist Bulgakov "plucks from the thicket of events all the comedy that always accompanies the contrasts and paradoxes of real life."[33] He emphasized the joyful episodes in the book, downplaying its bitter sarcasm.

Chapter Three
The Rise of a Satirist: Early Stories

Bulgakov's early writings consist of sketches, literary reportage, and short stories with a wide range. It should be noted that the unstable living conditions of the years 1922–26 compelled Bulgakov to work simultaneously on several short pieces and *The White Guard*. This explains the variety of genres in which he worked.

Most of the sketches published in the newspaper *Gudok* and in certain other papers and magazines are funny anecdotes prompted by the incongruities of life. Like Mikhail Zoshchenko's humorous stories, Bulgakov's sketches illustrate the everyday life of ordinary citizens in that peculiar period better than any history could.

Frequently Bulgakov did not choose topics for his sketches but based them on material sent by worker-reporters from various places. This dictated the narrative form: a kind of *skaz,* a stylized story utilizing the vocabulary and mentality of an ordinary worker. His major themes include the housing shortage and the nightmarish existence of overcrowded communal apartments. Other small events of everyday life, such as the malfunctions of the railroad system; abuse of working position; embezzlement; and compulsory visits by illiterate people to operas and concerts of classical music and other curious examples of "spreading culture among the masses"—all found a humorous interpretation from Bulgakov. Public meetings with speakers who used propagandistic clichés and foreign words which even they sometimes did not understand, as well as inept and confusing orders from local authorities, and multiple layers of bureaucracy also provided rich material for Bulgakov's satire.[1]

Sometimes the names of high Soviet functionaries cropped up—such as Anatoly Lunacharsky, Grigory Zinoviev, Lev Kamenev, and Nikolay Bukharin—adding a peculiar time coloration to these sketches.[2] Bulgakov reworked a few of his sketch topics into more sophisticated reportage for *Nakanune*. These feuilletons differ from the sketches in form and style, since in the feuilletons, Bulgakov addressed educated Russian emigrés living in Western Europe, but vitally interested in events in their homeland. Bulgakov saw it as his journalistic duty to inform them of Soviet life realistically, but still in his characteristically ironic manner.

Bulgakov described Moscow slowly recovering from the hardships caused by revolution, civil war, and a shattered economy. Shortages of everything, empty stores, dilapidated buildings, paper rubles counted in millions and billions, and a mad struggle for survival are described in the cycles *Redstoned Moscow,*[3] *Forty Times Forty,* and especially *Moscow in the Twenties.* One dominant theme, as we have seen in the semi-autobiographical feuilletons, is the housing shortage and the arbitrariness of the authorities, who evicted old tenants from their apartments or confiscated some of their rooms and settled strangers there.[4]

Many passages depicted *nepmen,* people who suddenly emerged after the proclamation of the "New Economic Policy," or "NEP." The *nepmen* hastened to profit from a short interval of government-condoned private enterprise and commerce. They filled reopened restaurants and theaters, enjoying good food, wine, women, and a relaxed atmosphere. Their existence misled some into believing there had been a return to prerevolutionary conditions.[5] The ambiguous NEP period was the setting for many of Bulgakov's stories and plays.

In a few stories—some published in *Nakanune,* others in the collection *Diaboliad*—Bulgakov resorted to fantastic grotesque to emphasize the absurdity of the unstable new bureaucracy. Two stories are characteristic for this trend—"Pokhozhdeniia Chickikova" ("The Adventures of Chichikov") and "Diavoliada" ("Diaboliad").

The first story is a fantasy on the theme of Gogol's *Dead Souls,* with incorporation of motifs and names from other works of his. Aside from extremely witty parallels between Gogolian and modern times, the story presents an ingenious amalgam of realistic description of postrevolutionary bureaucracy with Gogol's sentences, adjusted to contemporary conditions. Of course, to appreciate Bulgakov's stylistic virtuosity, the reader must recognize the Gogolian elements in Bulgakov's satire.

"The Adventures of Chichikov,"—"A Poem in Two Points with a Prologue and an Epilogue," as defined by the subtitle—is presented as the author's "bizarre dream."[6] In this grotesque parody,

Gogol's famous adventurer Pavel Chichikov, buyer of dead serfs, finds a marvelous opportunity for his machinations in Moscow of the NEP period. Nothing has changed since Gogol's times, the 1840s, except that the hotel Chichikov left one hundred years ago has been transformed into "Dormitory No. Such-and-such," and become even filthier. Chichikov quickly realizes that now, as in the past, everybody deceives everybody else, and he profits from the situation by building nonexistent enterprises, obtaining government loans, and earning astronomical sums of paper rubles by cheating in the export trade.

But suddenly Gogol's characters Nozdrev and Korobochka betray Chichikov. It becomes clear that he is "A Swindler" and an "investigation commission" is appointed to catch him. The author "emerges like some deus ex machina" and offers to handle the case. He ruthlessly catches Chichikov, orders that his stomach be slit open, and finds all the stolen diamonds and billions of rubles. As a reward the author thinks at first of asking for "Pants. . . . A pound of sugar. . . . A 25 watt bulb. . . ," but then recovers his "writer's dignity" and asks only for Gogol's complete works. And suddenly Gogol is on his desk! Unfortunately, the author soon awakens, with no Gogol or Chichikov in sight.

"Diaboliad" was completed in August 1923, and published in the almanac *Nedra* (1924). This satirical phantasmagoric story is firmly rooted in the real environment of that historic period.

During his job hunting at the beginning of his Moscow career, Bulgakov faced bureaucracy in all its absurdity, when the document replaced the individual, and establishments emerged and disappeared with fantastic rapidity, or were relocated without warning no one knew where. Bulgakov's brief employment with "LITO" provided him with rich material for his satire: the staff were paid in dry peas instead of money; and once, upon arriving two hours late for work, Bulgakov found an empty room. Only on the next day did he discover that "LITO" had been transferred to another part of the huge building. [7]

"Diaboliad" is subtitled "The Story of How Twins Destroyed a Clerk." Indeed, this funny story has a sad ending: laughable devilry is responsible for the suicide of a distraught young man. "Diaboliad" contains eleven short chapters, each describing a new step in Varfolomei Korotkov's phantasmagoric struggle for his position and his identity. The story begins with a description of the minor employee's situation and his illusory hopes of stability: "At the time when everyone was jumping from one job to another, Comrade Korotkov worked steadily at Macentsupmatmat [Main Central Supply of Matchmaking Materials] as a regular clerk—and he had served there for eleven whole months."[8]

The action occurs during one week in September 1921. On 20 September the cashier of "Macentsupmatmat" leaves the office to bring money for the employees' salary. As there is no money at the bank for him, three days later the employees are paid in kind, with matches.

Catastrophe occurs the next day, when a new director—a Goyan grotesque monster with a huge bald head named Kalsoner—fires Korotkov. All Korotkov's efforts to explain the situation to Kalsoner are fruitless; Comrade Kalsoner rushes with his shiny black briefcase purposelessly from one office to another, and Korotkov cannot reach him.

Now Korotkov is robbed of his wallet and his identification card, and becomes confused with a certain Vasily Kolobkov. The "demonic trick" expands. The bald Kalsoner splits in two, producing a second Kalsoner with a large beard, who takes Korotkov's place at the clerk's desk. Unable to bear the nightmarish "doubling," Korotkov attacks the bearded Kalsoner. A cinematic chase begins; the persecuted Korotkov finally tries to hold off his pursuers in a billiard room at the top of an eleven-story building. When his pursuers, armed with pistols and machine guns, surround him, Korotkov jumps from the roof, shouting "Better death than shame!"[9]

In this surrealistic satire Bulgakov used several comic devices, such as funny names, confusion of identities, sudden emergences and disappearances, and magic transformations. Thus the bearded second Kalsoner is metamorphosed into a black cat with phosphorescent eyes, and the presence of diabolic sorcery is suggested by the frequent presence of suffocating sulphurous odor. Korotkov searches vainly for the office of claims and complaints: he rushes to the right, but after a five-minute race through endless corridors he finds himself at the very spot from which he began. He then rushes to the left, with the same result. His life is caught in a vicious circle: "Don't run around, dear, you won't find it anyhow," a wrinkled old woman emerging from a secret door, a caricature of the death image, tells him. Another omen of despair and destruction appears in the figure of an old man who, at their first encounter, tells Korotkov that he has already crossed him "off the list."

A terrifying, Kafkaesque atmosphere of absurdity permeates this fantastic story, where the defects of routine bureaucracy take on the dimensions of a grotesque nightmare. The end of the story is not funny. The humble Korotkov literally fights for his identity and for his authentic place in life, but when he loses the unequal battle Korotkov casts himself into the "abyss," and self-destruction.

Two major stories of this period, "The Fatal Eggs" and *Heart of a Dog,* treat certain similar themes quite differently. In both stories popular science fiction subjects are embedded in the realistic environment of Moscow in the 1920s. While the realistic details of everyday Soviet life are described in Bulgakov's usual ironic manner, the presentation of two other themes—of the scientist and the fate of his discovery—goes far beyond the frame of jovial satire.

H. G. Wells's science fiction was popular at the time, but there was genuine scientific research on problems of biology and medicine, on many obscure phenomena of living organisms, going on then. Both Bulgakov's uncles were physicians, as he was himself, which made the scientific ambience familiar to him. The image of the old magician-scholar Doctor Faust, bent over his books and retorts, appealed to Bulgakov as a symbol of man's eternal striving after knowledge. But this also entails the danger of unleashing forces that can escape the scholar's control and cause evil.

The action of "The Fatal Eggs," written in 1924,[10] takes place in the space of five months in 1928, in Moscow and at the magnificent country estate of Count Sheremetiev, transformed into a Soviet farm. A famous zoologist and university professor, Vladimir Persikov, discovers a red, life-giving ray during one of his routine experiments with amoebas. Under the influence of this ray, the almost lifeless amoebas multiply rapidly and begin a furious struggle for a place in the ray.

With the help of his assistant Ivanov, Persikov continues his experiments with frog roe exposed to a thicker and more powerful ray in a larger chamber. Ivanov immediately traces a parallel between Persikov's discovery and the H. G. Wells novel *The Food of Gods,*[11] but Persikov rejects any connection: though he has read this novel, he has forgotten it completely. When news about the ray spreads in Moscow, Persikov is besieged by journalists. In June, Persikov interrupts his work to help the government suppress a chicken plague.

Only at the end of July may Persikov and Ivanov resume their experiments with the red ray, now with government aid. But Persikov's dream of a quiet scientific work is destroyed by a veteran of revolutionary battles, a resolute man with a revolver and the strange last name of Rokk, a homonym of the Russian word for fate. Appointed as director of a Soviet farm, Rokk decides to promote the revival of chicken breeding after the plague with the help of Persikov's ray. Through administrative error, the eggs of snakes, ostriches, and crocodiles are sent to the farm from abroad instead of chickens' eggs. Under the red ray, gigantic monsters hatch and destroy all the farm workers except Rokk, who manages to escape, then march upon Moscow. An indignant mob breaks into the Zoological Institute and brutally murders Persikov. A few days later a sudden frost, unusual in August, kills all the tropical monsters and saves Moscow.

The story is masterfully constructed: an ingenious plot, dynamic action, and suspense make it highly entertaining reading, as fantastic events merge with reality.

Bulgakov describes Professor Persikov with sympathetic humor. A brilliant scholar and a typical absent-minded professor, Persikov is totally absorbed by his zoological research, which has brought him international fame, but also caused his wife to abandon him as early as 1913. According to Bulgakov's second wife, several features of Persikov and his physical portrayal were suggested by a relative of hers. [12]

Backed by a governmental order, the incompetent, aggressive Rokk confiscates Persikov's chambers. This act of violence and the consequent misuse of Persikov's discovery unleash an incredible disaster. When Persikov and Ivanov realize what has happened, Persikov has a heart attack, for he feels responsible for the consequences of his discovery. Any bold experiment can lead to unexpectedly adverse results: that is the main idea of this story.

Critics of Bulgakov's day accused him of having produced a mocking allegory on the Bolshevik Revolution, and L. F. Ershov reiterated this accusation in 1960, characterizing "Bulgakov's phantasmagoria" as "a vicious pamphlet against Revolution." [13] Some Western critics have also emphasized its political aspect. However, in recent years more profound analysis has demonstrated the story's multivalence and its more universal relevance.[14]

Heart of a Dog, written in 1925, was destined for the almanac *Nedra,* but it was rejected. Bulgakov's second wife has recalled in her memoirs the "beautiful evening" when two "investigators" visited the Bulgakovs, and spent all night looking through books and manuscripts. When they found *Heart of a Dog* and Bulgakov's diaries, the "guests" confiscated them and left immediately. Only two years later, at Maxim Gorky's insistence, was the manuscript returned to the author. The story was first published in 1968, and only in the West.[15]

The plot is rather simple: Professor Filipp Preobrazhensky (one who transforms or transfigures), a famous Moscow surgeon and specialist on rejuvenation, is also well known abroad for his research on the human brain. One day he takes an injured stray mongrel, Sharik, for a bold experiment. He and his assistant, Dr. Ivan Bormental, replace Sharik's testes and pituitary gland with those of a man killed three hours earlier. The result is astounding: the operation transforms the dog into a human. Professor Preobrazhensky realizes that he has made an important discovery: that the pituitary hormones determine human characteristics. Consequently, Sharik becomes a vulgar, insolent proletarian, like Klim Chugunkin, whose pituitary he has received. This new "Comrade Sharikov" turns the professor's life into a nightmare, until finally he threatens his creators with a gun. Finally Preobrazhensky and his assistant perform another operation, returning Sharikov to his former shape as a dog.

The multilevel narrative exhibits Bulgakov's virtuosity in elaborating various themes. Different narrative "voices"—including Sharik's inner monologue at the beginning and at the end—contribute to an impressive blend of diverse elements which, to an extent, anticipates the structure of *The Master and Margarita.* Humor, biting social satire, bold political statements, grotesque images and situations exist alongside the mysterious world of scientific discovery.

Like Faust's disciple Wagner, Preobrazhensky and Bormental create a being that finally threatens to destroy its creators. Bulgakov asked an old friend from Kiev, then a Moscow surgeon, for advice on surgery and medical experiments.[16]

Preobrazhensky's patients view him as a wizard and magician; for Sharik he is a godlike benefactor and high priest; for Dr. Bormental he is the greatest scientist in Europe. Preobrazhensky does not read Soviet papers, dislikes the proletariat, and openly criticizes the new system, though he insists that his views are not "counterrevolutionary," but rather based on common sense (54–55). He is against terror and violence, believing, as he does, that "kindness is the only method possible in dealing with living creatures" (28).

Paradoxically, when Preobrazhensky operates on Sharik, he and Bormental use coercion: the dog sees in their eyes "something nasty, evil, something criminal." To be sure, any surgery is "violent," but this operation, described in clinical detail, is especially so. The two doctors are compared to vampires and tigers; they both looked like "hurrying murderers" (71). Everything connected with the creature they produce is vulgar, evil, and grotesque. In the figure of Sharikov, vile forces are unleashed that escape the doctors' control. In the end Preobrazhensky realizes that his discovery is in fact harmful, and declares that natural evolution is the only proper path of development (132–34). Otherwise we would be left with a grotesque paradox: Sharikov with a human heart is a nuisance with bestial instincts, while the dog Sharik possessed many almost human qualities. [17] Preobrazhensky corrects his "mistake," but his insatiable mind does not rest: he is soon contemplating a new experiment. Thus at the end the author returns to the ethical problem—the ambiguous nature of science, the close connection between good and evil. [18]

The short story "No. 13. Dom Elpit-Rabkommuna" ("No. 13. The Elpit-Rabkommun Building") describes a luxurious house previously belonging to Adolphe Elpit but now a "Workers' Commune," in which the new tenants ruin everything. "It is terrible to live when kingdoms are falling," the author comments half-ironically, half-objectively. [19]

In vain the former owner, who still hopes to repossess his property, and his loyal administrator Boris Khristi try to save the house by heating it. A four-day shortage of heating oil in a frosty February prompts an ignorant woman in one apartment to light her small iron stove: she places the stove pipe in the ventilation passage, taking it for a flue. The house promptly burns to the ground, causing several deaths.

The story "Khanskii ogon' " (Khan's fire) stands apart in Bulgakov's writings of that time, but also ends in fire. In "Elpit Workers' Commune" the fire is caused by the ignorant arrogance of uneducated people, but here the sumptuous palace of the Tugai-Beg princes, converted into a National Museum after the Revolution, is deliberately destroyed by the last of its former owners. The story is complex, with fine insight into human psychology with political overtones. The museum visitors look with indifference at the precious palace treasures for they have no connection with their interests. A grotesque half-naked visitor mocks its former owners and the Russian emperors whom the Tugai princes served over five hundred years. In the end the last prince, Anton Tugai, arrives incognito from abroad, and, to prevent the public denigration of his family and the falsification of their and Russia's past, sets fire to the wonderful palace.[20]

Several of Bulgakov's early stories concern the Civil War; some situations in them recall similar episodes described in *The White Guard,* which he was writing at the time.

"Krasnaia Korona" ("The Red Crown," 1922) contains several constant themes in Bulgakov's work. One is that of the guilty conscience. After a tragic event, a man realizes that he should have prevented it, but did not know how. And so remorse, the awareness of his guilt and responsibility, torture him day and night, clouding his mind. Reality and hallucination merge, turning his life into a nightmare.

Another important theme is that of protest against violence, the killing and torturing of men by other men. An impossible desire to repair the irreparable runs through "The Red Crown," and also Bulgakov's last work, *The Master and Margarita.*

"The Red Crown" is subtitled "Historia morbi." The narrator, a patient in a psychiatric ward, tells the story of his disease to himself, addressing, perhaps, also the doctor and nurses who had prevented his first suicide attempt. His illness is the result of two traumatic experiences. The first occurred when he involuntarily witnessed the hanging of a worker, in whose boot soldiers had found a certificate with a round blue seal proving his collaboration with the Reds. The narrator had been unable to prevent the hanging.

Kolya, the narrator's younger brother, was victimized by the Reds, on the other hand. A young cadet, he joined the Russian Volunteer Army in the South. His old mother, unable to live any longer in a state of anguish and fear, implored the narrator to find Kolya and bring him back alive. And the narrator found his brother in the ranks of a cavalry squadron on the way to a village under attack by the Reds. He tried to persuade Kolya to return home with him, but Kolya simply asked his brother to wait for him at the edge of a wood.

An hour later, Kolya returned with only two companions; his squadron had been annihilated by the Red troops. Kolya's pose surprised the narrator: "The horseman, my brother, in a shaggy red crown, sat motionless on the horse, and if the man on his right had not been supporting him carefully, one could have thought that he was going on parade."[21] Truly, it was Kolya's last parade: he had not deserted his squadron, but had performed his duty. Now, his eyes stained with blood, the crowned horseman returned every night to his elder brother, saying, "Brother, I can't leave my squadron."

The madness of the reality of men's senseless mutual extermination is perpetuated in the madness of hallucination. The narrator-patient cannot atone for his guilt, and he is unable to free himself from self-reproach for letting Kolya go off to battle. During the hour the battle lasted the Reds disfigured his brother, blinded him, and set a martyr's red crown upon his head.

This short story masterpiece embodies the unbearable torment of unfulfilled responsibility and inexpiable guilt. In this tragic work Bulgakov emerges as a great writer who grasped the most poignant ethical problems of modern times.

The same themes of murder and cruelty are at the core of the chapter "V noch' na 3-e chislo" (On the night of the third, 1922) from the unfinished novel *The Scarlet Stroke*.[22] The action takes place in Kiev and its suburb Slobodka, on the night of 3 February 1919, when Petliura's troops were withdrawing under Bolshevik pressure. The young doctor Mikhail Bakaleinikov was mobilized by Petliura's Army. On that icy-cold February night, he witnesses the harsh treatment of alleged deserters by Colonel Mashchenko and his soldiers of the Blue Division, and also sees Petliura's soldiers beating a Jew to death. Shocked, the doctor decides to escape. When, after a deadly chase, he miraculously survives to reach his house, his hair has turned white. He reproaches himself for his inability to halt the execution he has just witnessed.

"Nalet" ("The Raid," 1923), subtitled "In a Magic Lantern," takes place at a sentry post near a small railroad station one stormy winter night in the midst of Civil War. This story also centers around violence: the beating of the three guards on duty, apparently by Petliura's troops. Two of the sentries are Russians and one is a Jew. One of them is shot instantly by a cavalry detachment that suddenly appears. The two others, Streltsov and Abram, are beaten and then shot. The story is seen through Abram's eyes. Abram suddenly realizes that the small black mouth of the gun facing him is the end of everything.[23] He faints and does not hear the shot. When he regains his senses, he is badly wounded in the chest, but manages to reach a watchman's hut, where the frightened watchman's wife takes care of him.

The whole dramatic episode is presented impressionistically. Three lights pierced the snowstorm: the cold white light of the distant railroad station; a small yellowish one buried in the snowdrifts beyond the tracks; and a blinding flashlight in the hand of a horseman, which snatched from the black night, as in a nightmarish phantasmagory, now a horse's muzzle, now Streltsov's blood-stained face, now a black pistol. There was also the little yellow light of a kerosene lamp that showed Abram the way to the watchman's hut and saved his life.

Three years later, "Ia ubil" (I killed, 1926) takes up the same themes of atrocities and the absurdity of human hatred and violence. On the cold night of 2 February 1926, the hero of the story, Dr. Yashvin, tells the narrator, his colleague in a Moscow hospital, what had happened to him in Kiev exactly seven years earlier, in 1919, when Petliura's rule was coming to an end. Dr. Yashvin tried to continue "working toward his scientific degree in this mess."[24] He tried to leave Kiev, but was held up by Petliura's soldiers, and finally brought to a room where traces of blood were visible, and where a wounded cavalry officer, Colonel Leshchenko, needed treatment. While attending to the colonel, Dr. Yashvin heard someone being beaten in another room. Suddenly, a woman barged in exclaiming: "Why did you shoot my husband?" In response to the colonel's cynical answer, "We shot him because we wanted to!" the woman turned to the doctor, calling him a scoundrel and asking how he could assist someone who slaughtered innocent people. Then she spat in the colonel's face. Enraged, he ordered his soldiers to seize her and give her twenty-five lashes with a ramrod. With the terse words, "I apparently put one of the bullets into his mouth," the doctor ended his morbid tale of how he, a stalwart opponent of violence, had killed his "patient."

Chapter Four
History versus Man
The White Guard

Mikhail Bulgakov lived in the midst of crucial historical events which in the space of a few years drastically changed conditions throughout Imperial Russia, and which were especially complex in the Ukraine, more particularly in Kiev. Here the young doctor encountered history, which not only demanded immediate decisions but frequently destroyed life, or gave it an unexpected twist.

The intention of writing a story about the Civil War in Kiev apparently solidified in Bulgakov's mind during his sojourn in Kiev in 1918–19. Bulgakov began to realize his plan to write a novel after the death of his mother in 1922, and did more intensive work on it in 1923–24.

In May 1923 Bulgakov made a short trip to Kiev. What he saw in his beloved city, still shattered by recent turmoil, he described in his feuilleton "Kiev-gorod" (The city of Kiev)."[1] This humorously lyrical description of the city with its chestnuts and lindens turning green, the destroyed Chain Bridge, the ruins of the Pechersk district, and the inhabitants still dazed in their experiences, yet ends on a hopeful note: amid the carnage and destruction the writer detected a flicker of newborn life. Such observations found their way into *The White Guard.*

Bulgakov had in mind a long epic work, originally conceived as a trilogy, in which the fate of the Turbin family and their friends would be depicted against a vast panorama of the Civil War. In his 1924 autobiography, Bulgakov alluded rather imprecisely to the time he spent on his novel: "I wrote the novel *The White Guard* in one year. This novel I like more than any other of my works."[2]

In *The White Guard* Bulgakov reconstructed the history of 1918 and 1919. His skill in describing complex historical events is remarkable, even unique in Soviet literature of the 1920s. Bulgakov obviously sympathized with the Turbin family, but he objectively portrayed the struggle of several antagonistic groups: the right-wing

government of Hetman Skoropadsky; the national socialist direc-
torate of the Ukrainian National Union as personified by its commander in chief, Simon Petliura; and the Russian population and
the officer class, who wanted the unity of the Russian Empire restored. Hoping to publish the novel in Moscow, Bulgakov deliberately ended his story on 4–5 February 1919, on the eve of Kiev's
seizure by Red troops. Bolshevik power was personified in Leon
Trotsky, the creator of the Red Army and its commander in chief
then.

The novel moves on two distinct levels, the historical and the
personal. The peaceful life of the Turbin family is presented against
a historical background—they and their close friends have become
immediately involved in tumultuous events with an unpredictable
outcome. Amid the general confusion and dissolution of all traditional external ties, the family and honor alone survived.

The action of *The White Guard* takes place over only a few days,
but days of momentous historical import. The story begins on 12
December 1918, as sounds of gunfire filtered into the Turbins' cozy
apartment, announcing Petliura's advance as German troops
withdrew.

Petliura's forces held Kiev only until early February 1919. Red
troops then occupied Kiev, only to be ousted in August 1919 by
Denikin's Volunteer Army.[3]

The novel consists of three parts divided into twenty chapters.
Part 1 covers some three days in 1918—12, 13, 14 December and
the early morning of the fifteenth; part 2 depicts the activities of
some participants in the events that occurred on 13 and 14 December, especially the latter; part 3 describes the events of 15, 16, and
17 December, the date of Petliura's triumphant entry into Kiev.
Another day described in detail is 22 December, when Alexey Turbin's illness reached a critical point. The story then ends on 2
February 1919 when Petliura's forty-seven-day rule ended.

The lives of the Turbin brothers, Alexey and Nikolay, and their
close friends, were entangled in this complex historical struggle.
The brothers, their sister Elena—married to Captain Sergey Talberg, a member of the Hetman's war ministry—and the loyal maid
Anyuta still mourned the death of their adored mother in May, soon
after Alexey had returned home after years of military service. Although they tried to honor their mother's last request to "go on

living" and maintain their home's warm ambience and traditions, "their destiny would be suffering and death."[4]

On 12 December the Turbins' friends—Lieutenant Victor Myshlaevsky, First Lieutenant Leonid Shervinsky, a member of the Hetman's staff, and Second Lieutenant Fedor Stepanov, nicknamed "Karas" ("carp")—gathered at the Turbins' apartment to discuss the current situation. Captain Talberg had just left for Germany, after confiding the news of the German withdrawal to his wife. A new Russian volunteer mortar regiment was formed under the command of Colonel Malyshev to protect the city from Petliura, which Karas had already joined. Though Alexey Turbin, a military doctor, thought it was by then too late to form a Russian army, he also declared his willingness to enroll in the regiment.

The next day Alexey Turbin and his friends reported to the commander of the mortar regiment, which consisted mostly of cadets and students. It occupied the Alexandrovsky High School, where Alexey and his friends had spent their youth. Early in the morning of 14 December, Malyshev disbanded his regiment, since the Hetman had fled to Germany the night before. But, like most of Kiev's inhabitants, Alexey Turbin, who had been ordered to report to the regiment at 2:00 P.M., did not know what had happened. Colonel Malyshev, now in civilian clothes, told Alexey to return home while the streets were still passable.

In the meantime, Petliura's first cavalry regiment had entered the city and engaged in scattered fighting with small pockets of volunteer units. Among them were Nikolay Turbin and his twenty-eight cadets: their retreat was covered by Colonel Nai-Turs until his death. Meanwhile Alexey Turbin was gravely wounded while fleeing from Petliura's pursuing soldiers, and rescued by Julia Reiss, who brought him home the next morning. Typhus had aggravated Alexey's severe wound, and for several weeks he lay near death.

The novel ends on the night of 2 February 1919. For the first time since Alexey's illness, all of the friends were gathered again in the Turbins' dining room. The rumor spread that the Red troops were advancing rapidly; indeed, by nightfall Petliura's divisions had left the city. At the Darnitsa railroad station the armored train "Proletarian" was ready to move toward Kiev.

In this novel Bulgakov works by describing several events occurring simultaneously in different places. The author contrasts the last happy evening at the Turbin apartment with the fears of the landlord, engineer Vasily Lisovich, who tried to hide his most valuable possessions but was robbed by three bandits. This episode recreates the anarchy of that troubled period.

Along with scenes from private life, Bulgakov paints a majestic panorama of Kiev, mother of all Russian cities, which suddenly became the target of several antagonistic forces. Bulgakov narrates the story of Kiev's troubled times in the style and language of the old Russian epics. An example is his initial sentence: "Great and dreadful was the year of Our Lord 1918, of the revolution the second. . . ." (111).

With this striking affinity for the old Russian epics, Bulgakov's concept of the everflowing course of history recalls the biblical image of those dark days when men's sins aroused the wrath of God.[5] Bulgakov symbolized the events that he experienced and depicted in his novel by two planets, evening's pastoral Venus and quivering red Mars, and the apocalyptic prophecies of St. John. For Bulgakov the horrors that befell the majestic city were explained symbolically by the verse: "For the great day of His wrath is come; and who shall be able to stand." (Rev. 6:17). For Bulgakov this question was of prime importance: who could preserve high moral principles amid chaos, confusion, and outbursts of fanaticism?

For the Turbins and their friends the concept of honor was most important. Alexey Turbin strove for justice and honor, but saw these values suddenly devalued. The Germans, who supported Hetman Skoropadsky's government, broke their word: though they helped the Hetman and some of his staff officers to escape to Germany, they abandoned hundreds of Russian officers and cadets without informing them of the decision to withdraw.

The Turbins and their friends were indignant at these actions, but they still supported the Hetman's government and continued to fight for a strong Russian state. Like his officer friends, Alexey could not remain passive when Kiev was endangered. All of them performed their duties and remained at their assigned posts until the last moment.

Unfortunately, Alexey and his friends did not know of the severe measures the German military authorities had taken against the Ukrainian peasants to obtain provisions. Myshlaevsky was surprised to discover that almost all the men of a neighboring village had left to join Petliura. At the end, when Russian officers and volunteers realized that their loyalty and courage were useless, all they could do was to seek to preserve their own moral integrity and prevent a bloodbath. For example, immediately after the Hetman's escape Colonel Malyshev, the commander of the volunteer mortar regiment, disbanded it in order to save 200 young men of whom only a third were cadets, and the rest students, who did not all even know how to shoot.

The seventeen-year-old Nikolay knew that Petliura's forces greatly outnumbered the scattered Russian volunteer units. Nevertheless, the idea of shirking military duty never entered his mind. For Nikolay, honor and duty were the paramount, inviolable principles: "no one should break his word or life will become impossible" (247). He preferred to die if necessary rather than to betray others and dishonor himself.

Besides the loyalty and courage of honorable men, Bulgakov describes outrageous instances of negligence and betrayal on the part of the Hetman's forces. High-ranking officers fled from danger and disclaimed all responsibility for the results of their actions. First among them were Hetman Skoropadsky and his commander in chief, General Belokurov.

Finally, Alexey Turbin and his friends realized that it was impossible to reverse history. Anyone who wanted to survive the frequent changes of power had to find a new way of life. As a doctor of medicine, whose duty was to save lives instead of taking them, Alexey abhorred violence. The ending of the novel is open, providing no clue as to Alexey's fate.

The attitudes and aspirations of the young, naive Nikolay were revealed through a masterfully written indirect inner monologue. Nikolay understood well that what had happened on 14 December was a terrible catastrophe. He mourned the death of Colonel Nai-Turs, who was for him a genuine hero. But at the same time, the young man, for whom life had just begun, looked to the future, and realized that life must go on, because "everything passes—suffering, pain, blood, hunger, and pestilence" (348).

Leonid Shervinsky is the only one whose future can be foreseen. He was the last to leave the Hetman's palace after the Hetman's flight. Even before then Shervinsky had decided to end his military career as soon as "everything gets back to normal" and realize his long-cherished dream of pursuing an artistic career. After Petliura entered the city, Shervinsky, a powerful baritone, did become an artist at the Kramskoy Opera Studio.

The women in the novel—Elena and her maid Anyuta—embody goodness, beauty, tenderness, and a touching concern for other people; they uphold family traditions and guard the last vestiges of peace and calm in a time of turmoil. After the mother's death, Elena Turbin-Talberg became the central figure in the Turbin family. She created for all those around her such a warm and friendly atmosphere that her house became a magnet for the Turbins' friends. Her anxious wait for her husband on the evening of 12 December, and her even more intense and desperate vigil during the night of 14 December, when she and Nikolay thought that Alexey would never return, truly re-create the atmosphere of those days. Nothing then was certain; a man, leaving his house for but an hour, never knew if he would return.

Elena had moments of doubt, but they did not weaken her profound religious faith. When she understood from the doctor's evasive answers that only a miracle could save the life of the typhus-stricken Alexey, she went to her room to pray to the Holy Mother of God to intercede with Her Son for just such a miracle. During her fervent prayer, Elena had a vision: she saw Him whose mercy she sought "beside the open grave, arisen, merciful, and barefoot." And then she saw some unfamiliar red-and-yellow sandstone rocks and olive trees (333)[6] At that moment, in another room, her brother passed through the worst crisis and began to recover.

The White Guard abounds in symbols, omens, visions, and dreams, which allow the author to transcend reality and place events in a historical and prophetic context, while also revealing his protagonists' moral essence. The cream-colored drapes on the Turbins' windows, for example, seem to protect the peaceful family life and the individual's privacy amid the menacing elements and swirling events. This symbolic meaning of the cream-colored drapes was pointed out by Larion, the naive and awkward nephew from Zhitomir, who unexpectedly came to visit them.

Cultural values are also sacred. Valentine's cavatina from the opera *Faust,* the "Shipwright of Zaandam" (Peter the Great) painted on Dutch stove tiles, and Pushkin's novel *The Captain's Daughter* are "absolutely immortal" because they will remain long after the deaths of the Turbins, Talberg, and their contemporaries.

The sun appeared as a cosmic symbol of bloodshed. During a parade of Petliura's army, a bright blood-red sun suddenly burst through the gray sky, "as big as anyone had ever seen it in the

Ukraine" (314). After the parade, people feared reprisals by Petliura's military authorities against Russian officers, landlords, and Jews, because Petliura supported a socialist system and an independent Ukrainian people's republic. The first victims were the Russian officers and cadets; persecution of the Jews was foreshadowed by the absurd slaughter of the peaceful Yakov Feldman.

Dreams are also frequent in the novel: they reveal not only the inner state of mind and moral essence of the protagonists, but also foreshadow the future. Such are Alexey Turbin's dream on the night of 14 December and Elena's prophetic dream about Nikolay's fate. But that very night the Turbins' little neighbor, Petya Shcheglov, dreamed sweet dreams: he saw a glittering diamond ball, ran to it and clasped it in his arms. Hatred, struggle, and killing did not exist for the little boy, as they did not exist for the distant stars, the significance of which is inaccessible to man's finite comprehension. Bulgakov ends his novel with a question: why do men, who know they are mortal, not turn their eyes toward the stars? Why?

The question remained unanswered; men are unable to learn the wisdom of the stars and they continue on Earth their fratricidal struggles, causing suffering, pain, and grief.[7]

The Days of the Turbins

The impossibility of publishing *The White Guard* in book form prevented Bulgakov from carrying out his plan of creating a Civil War epic, but he did not abandon the subject entirely. The idea of writing a play on the subject came to Bulgakov as he was rereading the first few installments of his novel in the magazine *Rossiia*. Nostalgia and anxiety revived memories of that tragic and confused time: Bulgakov later re-created the moving story of how the visual image of a play emerges in a writer's mind in his *Theatrical Novel*.[8]

The play *The Days of the Turbins* is not a stage adaptation of *The White Guard*. It is a new work in which several similar themes have been elaborated independently.[9] A brief synopsis of the play will demonstrate these basic differences.

At the center of the four-act play are the Turbin brothers and their sister Elena. On a cold winter evening Alexey—a thirty-year-old artillery colonel and commander of the Volunteer Regiment—his brother Nikolka—and eighteen-year-old cadet—and their sister Elena, all anxiously await the return of Elena's husband Vladimir

Talberg, a staff colonel at Hetman Skoropadsky's headquarters. The appearance of the half-frozen Captain Victor Myshlaevsky, who has just spent twenty-four hours on duty outside the city, ushers the atmosphere of dramatic events into the cozy apartment. The unexpected arrival of Lariosik, a cousin from Zhitomir, provides comic relief before the tense atmosphere returns with the arrival of Colonel Talberg: the German troops are about to abandon the city to its fate, and Talberg is leaving for Berlin. The brothers are shocked by Talberg's cowardice and egotism.

The Turbins and their friends—the newly arrived Lieutenant Shervinsky, formerly of Her Majesty's Uhlan Regiment but now personal aide to the Hetman, and Captain Studzinsky—all sit down at the dining-room table for what Nikolay prophetically calls the "Regiment's last meal," because the Regiment must go into action the next day. After patriotic songs and toasts to the czar, Alexey describes the dangerous situation: he sees only two major opposing forces—the White Volunteer Army and the Bolsheviks. Later, finding Elena alone in the dining room, Shervinsky speaks to her of his love.

The next evening, in act 2, Shervinsky is on duty in the Hetman's palace. To his surprise, he learns that the commander of the Volunteer Army has left for Germany with some officers of the headquarters staff. Instead of meeting with his staff as scheduled for that evening, Hetman Skoropadsky is urged by two German officers to go to Germany because Petliura's army is advancing and the situation is critical. Shervinsky calls Alexey Turbin to report that the Hetman has left the city. The second scene of act 2 shows Petliura's First Cavalry Division headquarters commanded by Colonel Bolbotun, a few moments before the start of the drive in Kiev.

The first scene of act 3 is the dramatic climax of the play. Alexey, in the majestic hall of Alexandrovsky High School, disbands his regiment but waits for the return of the recalled support men. Nikolay stays with him. As Petliura's horsemen approach, a shell burst kills Alexey. Nikolay is wounded by Bolbutun's soldiers but manages to escape.

In act 4, set on the Eve of the Epiphany, all the friends are again gathered at the Turbins'. Nikolka is crippled; Petliura's troops are withdrawing from the city as the Reds advance. Shervinsky has just had an audition at the opera where he was accepted as a singer. Elena consents to marry him. Talberg appears unexpectedly but is told of Elena's decision to divorce him and urged to leave. Myshlaevsky welcomes the advance of the Red troops.

The dates in the play do not correspond exactly to the historical dates of the actual events as depicted in the novel, although the chronological sequence is retained. A remark to the play says that the first, second, and third acts take place sometime in the winter of 1918, in other words during Petliura's advance on Kiev. Act 4 takes place two months later, on the Eve of the Epiphany, when, according to old Russian tradition, the Christmas tree candles are lit for the last time. The interval between acts 3 and 4 intensifies the dramatic tension and shows what drastic changes have occurred in the Turbin apartment with its cream-colored drapes, where the family still tries to preserve tradition.

Comparison of the novel with the play as it was, and still is, produced by the Moscow Art Theater, makes it evident that the play emphasizes the political approach. The first version of the play, still entitled *The White Guard* and written in the spring and summer of 1925, retained the major theme of the novel, that is, an investigation of the attitudes of those people who supported the old regime and old way of life amid the unpredictable events that crushed the old system and imposed drastic changes of ways of life. Myshlaevsky and Larion occupy far more important places in the play than in the novel. In the first version of the play, all three major proponents of White Guard principles and ideas—Alexey Turbin, Malyshev, and Nai-Turs—are present. However, the dynamics of the play called for further concentration. At the suggestion of the actor and producer Ilya Sudakov, the roles of the military physician Dr. Turbin and Colonel Malyshev were incorporated into one character,[10] it is now Colonel Alexey Turbin who is entrusted with the formation of the Volunteer Regiment, and who remains at his post to die a hero's death.

It is evident now that, during the long and painful process of creating an acceptable version, several major changes were made at the request of the producers and against Bulgakov's wishes. Although Bulgakov wanted to retain the title *The White Guard,* he proposed several others—such as *White December, 1918, Seizure of the City,* and *White Blizzard* but rejected *Before the End,* proposed by the Art Theater repertory commission. Stanislavsky knew that the inclusion of the word "white" in the title would cause the play to be banned, and eventually the final title was adopted.[11]

At the very beginning of the play, the comfort and security of the Turbin apartment—a fire in the fireplace and a Boccherini minuet—are suddenly interrupted: the electricity goes off and a distant cannon shot announces the danger of the moment.

The late supper, the "Regiment's last meal," with its brilliant dialogue between the naive teetotaler Larion and the resolute Captain Myshlaevsky, as well as a beautiful ballad of Pushkin's and a toast of the adorable Elena, revive for a moment the harmonious and peaceful life of the past.

For the first time in seven years, officers of the old czarist army appeared on stage in a Soviet theater as decent human beings instead of vile enemies. In 1968, the theater critic Konstantin Rudnitsky hailed the return of *The Days of the Turbins* to the Art Theater, commenting that "The Turbins signified nobility, intellectuality, the beauty of human relations, bravery, and perseverance."[12]

Alexey Turbin is the central figure of the play, the epitome of the courageous man who will never betray his oath. In the climactic scene at the Alexandrovsky High School, with its majestic marble staircase and the portrait of Emperor Alexander I watching the battle of Borodino, Alexey proves a resolute and brave commander. He disbands the Volunteer Regiment because, he says, "During the night in our position, in the situation of the entire Russian Army, and I would say, in the government position of the Ukraine sharp and sudden changes have occurred. . . . The battle with Petliura is over."[13] However, Turbin's statement that "it is the end of the White movement in the Ukraine" is historically inaccurate, and was apparently introduced to make the play acceptable to the Repertory Committee. In fact, in the winter of 1918–19, General Denikin's army became stronger and by June 1919 held the Crimea, the Don district, and part of the Ukraine. In August Denikin's units entered Kiev. However, in the play a total collapse underlines Alexey's determination to remain loyal to his convictions.

Alexey is determined to cover the escape of the last cadets from a small support unit by himself, and even sends Myshlaevsky away. Only Nikolka disobeys his order because he suspects his brother wishes to die, and so he does, faithful to his cause, although he knows his death cannot save it. Nikolay remains at the side of his brother and commander. Though wounded, he does not surrender, but manages to escape.

The pompous entrance of Bolbotun's troops in colorful uniforms, the deafening march, the national banners, and the loud, triumphant songs and shouts of "Glory, glory!" demonstrate the might of Petliura's forces, thus confirming Alexey's refusal to confront them.

Captain Studzinsky, a patriotic officer of the old school, cannot compromise with his conscience. Ever ready to defend the Russian Empire, and to fight against Petliura's troops, along with Alexey he still refuses to toast the Hetman's health during the last dinner at the Turbins': the Hetman's indecisive policy is unacceptable to them. Studzinsky will remain in the ranks of the White Guard until the bitter end.

His friend, Captain Myshlaevsky, chooses a different way. Myshlaevsky is the consummate professional soldier: he spent four years at the front and has continued to serve in the Hetman's army. Myshlaevsky is also an honest rebel, who cannot tolerate injustice, but even so his declaration of sympathy for the Reds at the end is quite unconvincing. He does not know them, and has to be told by Larion that Bolsheviks and Communists are the same. More understandable is his desire to continue serving in the Russian Army, even under Bolshevik command. This consideration indeed motivated the actions of many former czarist officers, who served in the Red Army when the danger of foreign occupation arose in 1919–20.

Along with honor, two other values—love and art—survive all historical upheavals. Shervinsky's artistic temperament, his love for Elena, roses, and music presage, from the first moment of his appearance on stage, a possible break in his career. Elena told him that he should become an opera singer. Two months later, Shervinsky, now a singer in the Opera Theater, asked Elena to marry him. She would continue to accompany him on the piano, and keep the Turbin traditions alive.

The play premiered on 5 October 1926. Its enormous success was due to its immediacy—the memory of the recent upheavals was still fresh in the minds of the spectators—as well as to its theatrical qualities and dramatic tension. Vladimir Nemirovich-Danchenko wrote that Bulgakov's "ability to develop a plot, to hold the audience in suspense during the entire performance, to create lifelike characters, and to lead the spectators to a sharply delineated conclusion is absolutely exceptional."[14]

The *Days of the Turbins* was staged exclusively at the Moscow Art Theater, and only for three seasons, before all Bulgakov's plays were banned in June 1929. In early 1932 performances of *The Days of the Turbins* were resumed with great success until 1941, when all its props and settings were burned during the bombardment of Minsk, where the Art Theater was on tour. The play was restaged in various theaters in the 1950s, and at the Art Theater in 1968. The most detailed analysis of the 1968 production was offered by the theater critic Konstantin Rudnitsky; he recalled that the first production of *The Days of the Turbins* "enjoyed the special fondness of Moscow theatergoers,"[15] but went on to say that it was pointless to compare the 1926 and 1968 productions: in 1926 *The Days of the Turbins* was a play of burning significance, but by 1968 it had become a historic drama of Russian intellectuals involved in the Civil War.

Flight

The theme of the Civil War is also central to the play *Beg (Flight)*, on which Bulgakov worked in 1927–28. It depicts the decisive phase of the Civil War, when the center of military activity shifted to the south of Russia, to the Ukraine and the Crimea, and when Red Army units commanded by M. V. Frunze began their offensive against Baron Petr Wrangel's White Army at the end of October 1920. *Flight* resumes the story of events about a year and a half after *The Days of the Turbins* ends.

In *Flight*, as in *The White Guard*, Bulgakov is very accurate in his description of historical events. He consulted several works on the final months of the struggle between Red and White forces in southern Russia and the Crimea, including two books by Yakov Slashchov, and studied the map of Tavrida and the Crimea. The geographical names mentioned in the play are actual places in the northern Tavrida and the Crimea, important strategic points and scenes of fierce battles.

In this play, Bulgakov expressed anew his concern with the destinies of people involved in great historic upheavals, as well as with man's inescapable responsibility for his own acts and attitudes in crisis situations. In addition to the combatants, who at one time at least had chosen the side they would support, intellectuals and members of the Russian nobility were also drawn haphazardly into the Civil War. During this period many Russian officers felt their duty lay in loyalty to their military oath, and they remained in the ranks of the White Army.

The action in *Flight* spans a year, from October 1920 to late autumn 1921. At first, the action takes place in the northern Tavrida, in southern Russia; then in the Crimea—in the northern part of the peninsula, and then in Sebastopol, the major Black Sea port. Later, the action shifts to Constantinople, with General Wrangel, who appears on stage as commander in chief of the Russian Volunteer Army.

Fast-changing events and uncertain situations, when at every moment human lives are threatened by uncontrollable incidents and arbitrary commanders, create an atmosphere of near phantasmagoria. To accentuate the irrationality of events, Bulgakov employs special techniques: everything that happens seems more like a nightmare than real life. The author's creative intent is clearly revealed by the play's subtitle, "Eight dreams," and the division of the four acts of the play into eight dreamlike episodes.

The military situation in the south reached a turning point on 27 March 1920, when Red troops captured Novorossiisk, a port on the Black Sea. When General Wrangel accepted appointment as commander in chief, the White Army was cut off from the mainland. Its Crimean forces totaled only about 50,000 men when the Reds prepared a massive assault. After some successful military operations in the northern Tavrida and the Kuban' region, which almost restored normal life in Sebastopol, then inundated with refugees, the situation began to deteriorate. After the Soviet authorities signed a provisional peace treaty with Poland on 12 October 1920, several armies, including Budenny's First Cavalry Army, were sent against Wrangel in Tavrida.

On 7 November the Reds assaulted the Perekop Isthmus where a major battle ended in the defeat of White Cossack troops, who were defending this main gateway to the Crimea. After the Perekop and Chongar fortifications were taken by the Reds, General Wrangel began to prepare for retreat, realizing that the situation was hopeless. His precautionary measures enabled all White Army units to reach Black Sea ports for evacuation along with a great number of civilians on naval and merchant vessels. On 11 November 1920, Wrangel issued a proclamation in Sebastopol ordering "the evacuation and embarkation at the Crimean ports of all those who are following the Russian Army on the road to Calvary."[16] Wrangel was the last to leave the pier in Sebastopol as "the fleet, numbering a hundred and twenty-six ships, and carrying 145,693 men, women, and children in all, turned westward for Constantinople,"[17] in the words of a historian. This military, political, and personal tragedy found artistic incarnation in *Flight*.

The first act of *Flight* contains two dreams. Dream One takes place in a monastery in Northern Tavrida, when the territory is suddenly invaded by a small Red cavalry unit. Everybody seeks refuge in the church; among them are the archbishop of Simferopol, the young scholar Sergey Golubkov, the typhus-stricken Serafima, and General Charnota, disguised as a woman, whose own hussars break through and retake the territory. Dream Two takes place at General Khludov's headquarters at a railroad station in the northern Crimea.[18] Khludov attempts to maintain discipline in the already desperate situation and to assert his power by means of severe punishments. The delirious Serafima and Krapilin, Charnota's orderly, accuse Khludov of cruelty; Khludov orders Krapilin hanged. The commander in chief orders the troops to cease resistance to the Reds.

The second act includes two dreams. Dream Three takes place in a counterintelligence office in Sebastopol: Serafima is suspected of being a Communist agent, and is interrogated along with Golubkov. The setting of Dream Four is an office of the chief's headquarters in Sebastopol, where everybody is being brought aboard ships.

The third act takes place in Constantinople. A plaza with a carrousel emerges in Dream Five; Charnota is peddling toys on the street, and his attempt to win money gambling on cockroach races fails. Penniless, he returns, in Dream Six, to the poor house where he has already lived for six months with Serafima and his mistress Liuska in extreme poverty. Golubkov and Charnota leave for Paris to ask Korzukhin, Serafima's husband, for help.

In the fourth act, Dream Seven shows Golubkov and Charnota in Korzukhin's luxurious villa in Paris. Charnota plays cards with Korzukhin and wins $20,000. Unexpectedly Liuska appears as the future Madame Korzukhina. Dream Eight returns the action to Constantinople. When Golubkov and Charnota reappear, Serafima and Golubkov decide to go back to Russia on a ship sailing that very night for the Crimea. Khludov also returns to face punishment for his crimes, but Charnota chooses to stay abroad.

Flight is theatrical in the highest degree. Its fade-out, fade-in techniques, action scenes, music, symbolic songs, sound, and lighting effects as suggested in the playwright's remarks to each dream, give producers rich opportunities. The Russian title, *Beg,* has multiple meanings, expressing the ideas of flight, running, and racing. The epigraph, taken from a famous poem by the romantic poet Vasily Zhukovsky, suggests a philosophical and ethical concept of human life as a race to the finish—to another world, and perhaps to immortality, which shines like the lights on a silent, distant shore, to which man aspires throughout his life. All episodes of the play, which is built around real events and people, contains also another and more profound significance in the guise of a metaphor. Behind the concrete actions of each protagonist, the playwright suggests the universal meaning of Man in his clash with history.

The play begins and ends with Serafima and Sergey Golubkov, whose flight into chaos and the unknown is unplanned and uncontrollable. For Serafima and Golubkov the only escape from poverty, illness, sorrow, and grief lies in their past, reexamined and reinterpreted in a romantic and idealized sense. Unfortunately, they ignore the fact that no one can act "as if nothing had ever happened."[19] The home for which they long is no longer the same, and their native St. Petersburg has changed drastically during their absence.

Though the story of Serafima and Golubkov is the main plot, the central figure of the play is Roman Khludov, commander of the Southern front. In Khludov Bulgakov created an artistic image of a strong man whose despair over the imminent defeat of the entire cause for which he had courageously fought made him resort to cruelty. His conflict with reality deepened into an incurable moral sickness: he hanged anyone he suspected of being the enemy.

The theme of killing people caught up in events away from the battlefield occurs at the very beginning of the play, with the appearance of Baiev, Budenny's regimental commander. After breaking through the White lines, Baiev storms into the monastery church cursing and threatening the monks. Seeing a flickering light which he mistakes for a signal, Baiev shouts: "Just wait, if I find anything in the bell tower, I will line you up against the wall, every one of you, together with your old gray devil [the aged Father Superior]!" (129–30).

The theme of cruelty also becomes Khludov's leitmotiv. He threatens to hang a panic-stricken stationmaster if an armored train does not pass through in fifteen minues, although he knows that all the tracks are jammed. After Khludov's absurd order to arrest the delirious Serafima for her outburst of despair, Khludov hangs the taciturn soldier Krapilin, who has accused him of cruelty, seeing in him a kind of apocalyptical monster (153). Khludov's next order is to put everyone in his headquarters on the trains, then instruct the armored train to destroy everything left behind. Thereafter Krapilin's ghost will not leave Khludov's side.

In Khludov Bulgakov has put on stage a man who had committed crimes in a paroxysm of despair over an imminent defeat. But his conscience has recovered its voice: Khludov's decision to return to Soviet Russia, where he is sure to be shot, is motivated by his search for redemption. He has undergone his own trial and pronounced his own verdict.

Major General Grigory Charnota, born a Zaporozhian Cossack, is quite another sort of man. A brave fighter, a professional military man, Charnota is capable of marching into mortal combat to the strains of a tender ballroom waltz. Charnota is also an honest man. Upon his arrival at the railroad station after the fierce battle at the Chongar Gorge, Charnota urges Khludov to cease his cruelties, only to be sent into another battle. When, in Sebastopol, he miraculously hears Serafima's cry for help, he bursts into the counterintelligence office and frees her forcibly, an action that ultimately led to his discharge from the army. Charnota is a gambler—he enjoys risk both on the battlefield and at the card table.

Charnota is also a great patriot: he can never forget his native Ukraine, and Kiev. However, he sees reality without a romantic veil; he refuses to return to Soviet Russia with Khludov because, although he is proud of never having run from death, he does not want "to make a special trip for it to the Bolsheviks" (212). Wherever he lives in exile, he will take life as it is, and never surrender his basic principles.

Paramon Korzukhin, former deputy minister of commerce, is the real villain of the play. He was not subject to any danger in combat; his actions were motivated by a consuming interest in his own well-being. His major sin is cowardice: he rejects his wife Serafima when he feels that his safety could be endangered if he recognized her as his wife at Khludov's inquiry. He lives at ease in his luxurious villa in Paris as a French citizen and successful businessman, and experiences no remorse. In Korzukhin Bulgakov created a sharply satirical figure of an egotist.

Unfortunately Bulgakov never saw *Flight* staged during his lifetime. The Art Theater could never overcome the resistance of the authorities.

After the revival of *The Days of the Turbins* in 1954, several theaters turned to *Flight:* according to official statistics of 1968, *Flight* had by then been performed 202 times in fifteen theaters in the Soviet Union.[20] These productions generated many articles and reviews which sought to evaluate the play relatively objectively. While many Soviet reviewers, as one might expect, emphasized the political aspect of the play, Western scholars analyzed its artistic and ethical values. Ellendea Proffer has commented that to read this play simply as a political statement "is to ignore its central theme: the ways in which one group of people react to the violent disintegration of their world."[21] And Mirra Ginsburg maintains that Khludov's nightmarish experience is the drama of a man "who is both executioner and victim" through the dissolution of moral standards and restraints.[22]

Chapter Five
The Development
of a Playwright

The short period between 1925 and 1930 saw Bulgakov the playwright at the height of his powers. Finally he seemed to have realized his Caucasian dream: to write plays and see them performed in Moscow by first-rate actors. During the staging of *The Turbins,* in 1925, Bulgakov wrote the comedy *Zoika's Apartment.* In 1927, along with the drama *Flight,* he wrote a comedy, *The Crimson Island,* and in 1931 a fantastic comedy, *Adam and Eve.* In spite of the banning of all his plays in 1929, Bulgakov continued to work on *Bliss,* another fantastic comedy. Thus, in 1928 he reached the peak of his theatrical career: three of his plays were staged by three prominent Moscow theaters.

Zoika's Apartment

According to the memoirs of Bulgakov's second wife, the playwright took the subject for *Zoika's Apartment* from a local newspaper. The Soviet militia had discovered a gambling den concealed as a fashion shop in the apartment of a certain Zoia Buialsky.[1] Bulgakov fleshed out these facts in his semi-autobiographical *Theatrical Novel,* in describing Maksudov's creative work. Sitting alone in his shabby room, Maksudov heard every evening the sounds of a waltz through the floor: "I thought, for instance, that there was an opium den downstairs and I even strung together something which I vaguely thought of as act 3. It had blue smoke, a woman with an asymmetrical face, a frock-coated opium addict, and a man with a lemon face and a squint who was creeping up on him with a sharp Finnish knife. A blow with the knife, a stream of blood. . . ."[2] And indeed such a scene takes place in act 4 of *Zoika's Apartment,* which continues the theme of Moscow of the 1920s, when life was full of grotesque and tragic incongruities.

Work on *Zoika's Apartment* began in the fall of 1925, and in January 1926 Bulgakov read it at the Art Theater Studio (later renamed the Vakhtangov Theater). It was approved and staged as a satire on the "NEPmen"—the new social group of enterprisers and managers who were allowed by the government to develop private initiative to help stabilize the country's badly shaken economy. It opened at the Vakhtangov Theater on 28 October 1926, three weeks after *The Days of the Turbins* had premiered at the Moscow Art Theater.[3]

The play consists of four acts; except for one scene, the action takes place in Zoika's apartment. The huge house is overcrowded; all kinds of sounds, "a hellish concert" suggesting disharmony and trouble, fill Zoika's living room through the open window on a May evening. Zoika, an attractive young widow, needs money to go to France with her lover, the former Count Obolianinov. By bribing the chairman of the House Committee, Zoika tries to save her comfortable six-room apartment from forcible occupation by strangers sent by the House Committee. Goos ("Gus"), a powerful party man and commercial director of the Refractory Metals Trust, helps her obtain a permit to open a dress shop to make clothes for working women. Soon, through the active cooperation of Ametistov, Zoika's former adventurer friend, the dress shop becomes a fashionable rendezvous.

Modern dances, music, elegant women, liquor drinking, and occasional opium smoking created on stage a setting for a dream-world unattainable for most Soviet citizens at that time. Several other personages—for example, Goos's former mistress, the beautiful Alla, whose fiancé was in Paris; the picaresque adventurer Ametistov, Zoika's "cousin" and talented manager of her enterprise; and the Chinaman Cherubin—all dreamed of going abroad. Their hopes were destroyed by the secret police, whose agents had spotted the evening activities at Zoika's apartment and arrested Zoika and Obolianinov. Ametistov managed to escape after having found out that the Chinaman had robbed and killed Goos in order to return to Shanghai.

Everything in this play has a touch of illusion. Under an apparently futile, frequently comic, surface, a genuine human tragedy is revealed. Constant danger hangs over these people, who try to find temporary oblivion in Zoika's apartment.

Zoika and Ametistov knew that the evening activities of their dress shop, including demonstrations with live models, were in many ways illegal, but they took the risk. Zoika assured Obolianinov that they would be in Paris by Christmas, because she hoped to earn one million francs in six months.[4] Count Obolianinov accepted Zoika's project because, as he said, "It didn't matter" to him: he felt doomed in any case.

In the meantime, the "unslumbering eye" of Alilluya-Portupeya and his House Committee was constantly watching Zoika's apartment while she tried to bribe Alilluya to keep silent until Christmas. However, his insatiable greed foreshadowed the danger of denunciation and reprisals. The end of Zoika's apartment was precipitated by her factotum Maniushka and the rivalry of two Chinese men, Cherubin and Gan-Dza-Lin, who both wanted to marry Maniushka: Gan-Dza-Lin denounced Cherubin to the plainclothes policemen who came to inspect the apartment.

If Zoika is not really the play's central character, she is its driving force. An energetic, resolute woman, Zoika quickly adjusts to the atmosphere of the NEP period. Her atelier for fashion-crazy women is her practical response to the demands of the new party and bureaucratic elite.

Zoika defends herself against the pressures of the House Committee: she discovers the power of an official certificate issued by the Soviet authorities, and finds ways to equip herself with them. However, along with her practicality and "devilish" traits, Zoika also displays feminine, sympathetic features such as her love for the helpless Count Obolianinov and her readiness to use her connections with the powerful Goos to obtain exit visas for Alla and Ametistov. Obolianinov psychologically continues to live in the past, and now seeks escape in music, and in a dream of immigration to Nizza, a dream that his mistress Zoika attempts to realize.

Alexander Tarasovich Ametistov's character contrasts sharply with Obolianinov's. He is the eternal adventurer, gambler, and boaster, full of energy and enterprising spirit, devoid of moral principle, quick and witty, a swindler, but not a criminal. A virtuoso liar, Ametistov creates in a second an "impressive" life in the past: to Obolianinov he speaks of his nobleman's wealth and his estates; to the House Committee chairman, of his affiliation with the Communist party; to Boris Goos, of his alleged anthropological studies in Shanghai.[5]

The play unfolds in an atmosphere of carnivalesque ambivalence: everything and everybody has double or even triple faces. Thus, Zoika's apartment is her home, a dress shop by day, and then a night club. The "honest" Gan-Dza-Lin's laundry is a typical Chinese laundry, but at the same time a front for a well-organized drug trade. Maniushka figures as a maid, a niece, a model, and finally as the bride of the Chinese "Cherub," who, despite his angelic face, is a cold-blooded murderer and reckless drug pusher.

Boris Goos is the only character to retain his identity throughout the play. A typical character of the NEP period, a commercial director of a trust with substantial financial resources, Goos could not resist the temptations of a powerful position. He embodies Soviet corruption of the NEP period.

When staged, the play enjoyed a lasting success, and was performed almost two hundred times, despite fierce attacks from critics. But early in 1929 it was suspended and in 1960 its producer, Alexey Popov, repudiated this play as one in which the stage realization allegedly followed a direction opposite to the theater's intention.[6]

The Crimson Island

Bulgakov began working on his satirical comedy *The Crimson Island* in 1927, delivering it on 14 March 1927 to the prestigious Kamerny Theater, under its famous director Alexander Tairov.[7] *The Crimson Island* premiered on 11 December 1928.

Bulgakov's play presents a curious combination of buffoonery and lampoon with lyrical and tragic touches. Several subjects are parodied in this multileveled comedy. The first target of Bulgakov's parody is censorship, which gives unlimited power to a few individuals over the theater. Their omnipotence engenders the hypocrisy, obsequiousness, and rampant flattery displayed by the theater director Gennady. Paradoxically, Gennady is motivated by the best of intentions: he must save the theater and himself, and he supports a helpless playwright who cannot defend himself and his work. The presence of the victimized playwright on stage lends a tragic note to this witty play.

The idea of the play came from a short story, "The Crimson Island," which Bulgakov had published in *Nakanune* for 20 April 1924. Bulgakov presented the story as "a novel by comrade Jules Verne, translated from French into Aesopian by Mikhail Bulgakov." Using the names of Jules Verne's science fiction protagonists, such as Lord Glenarvan, Captain Hatteras, and Paganel, Bulgakov wrote a burlesque parody of propagandistic works on the Civil War and the seizure of power by the exploited masses. In the play *The Crimson Island,* Bulgakov made his early comic story the subject of the play written by his protagonist Vasily Arturovich Dymogatsky.

The Crimson Island is unique in its genre and structural complexity; it presents a curious example of a created illusion constantly shattered by the author in order to involve the audience more deeply in another illusion developing on the same stage and, through these techniques, to express implicitly the author's main concern and his central topic.[8]

Bulgakov's comedy consists of a prologue, four acts, and an epilogue. The subtitle—"A dress rehearsal of a play by Citizen Jules Verne in Gennady Panfilovich's theater, with music, the eruption of a volcano, and English sailors"—immediately emphasizes the experiences and procedures of producing the play rather than the play itself. A brief description of the places of action underlines the two levels on which the play moves. In the prologue the stage appears in its working state, as Gennady Panfilovich attempts to obtain approval for Dymogatsky's play, also entitled *The Crimson Island,* from the censor, a certain Savva Lukich, a member of the Main Repertory Committee that regulates playwrights and producers.

Dymogatsky's play was accepted for production with some changes, and Dymogatsky received 500 rubles from Gennady. When he brings the "corrected" text three days after the deadline, he finds Gennady in despair because Savva Lukich is going on vacation to the Crimea. The only way to save the theater's season schedule is to pretend that the play is ready for staging and to invite Savva Lukich immediately to a dress rehearsal. Savva Lukich promises to come, and the entire troupe hastens to perform a play they had never read.

Dymogatsky's play is a comic story of a revolt on an exotic island of the local population divided into two groups—the "white Moors" and "red Moors"—who fought against each other and, later on, the British merchant Lord Glenarvan, who wanted to buy the Moors' pearls at a very low price. Savva, who arrives in the middle of the third act, praises that act, in which some of the captive Moors escape from Lord Glenarvan's mansion in England. In the fourth act of Dymogatsky's comedy, all the Moors unite and force the English merchant ship to leave. But then unexpectedly, in the epilogue, Savva, who watched the fourth act from the former Moors ruler's throne on the top of the volcano, decrees that Dymogatsky's play "has been banned."[9] Finally, Gennady adds a "revolutionary" ending (the English sailors rebel and join the Moors), and thus rescues the entire performance.

Bulgakov took great liberties with Jules Verne's heroes in his play. Thus the noble and helpful Lord Glenarvan from *Les Enfants du Capitaine Grant* (The children of captain Grant, 1868) became the implacable "imperialist" who robs the innocent natives by exchanging cheap trousers, calico, and barrels of "fire-water" for their precious pearls. His sister Helena has been replaced by the capricious Lady Glenarvan, an unfaithful wife.[10]

In *The Crimson Island* the action develops simultaneously on different levels; all the protagonists play double roles, and the audience is constantly reminded that the actors are members of Gennady's theater troupe as well as protagonists of Dymogatsky's exotic play. Even the theater itself has two sides. Gennady constantly tells his actors that "The theater is a temple," but the disgruntled actress Adelaida calls it a "place of intrigues."

Unlike the classical play within a play, where actions developing on two different levels are visibly separated (as, for example, in Chekhov's *Seagull*), in *The Crimson Island* the action is constantly intermingled, and the boundaries between different levels are frequently destroyed. Bulgakov's techniques are similar to those used by Shakespeare in *A Midsummer Night's Dream* or by Molière in *L'Impromptu de Versailles*. However, Bulgakov's play is structurally more complex and masterfully superimposes the different levels so that theater and life converge.

The character of Savva Lukich incorporates all the negative features of governmental control over art. Bulgakov's second wife recalled that Savva Lukich was made up to resemble Blium, a powerful member of the Main Repertory Committee and one of Bulgakov's implacable foes.[11]

The theater director Gennady Panfilovich, who plays the part of Lord Glenarvan, calls himself "an old idealist" who dreams of a renaissance of the theater, but also knows that his theater must adjust to all unpredictable circumstances and the censors' absurd demands. That is why his mood and his behavior change with astonishing rapidity: a friend of his characterizes him as "quick as a deer." Gennady also knows that only a "highly ideological play" has a chance of being released for performance, but even he does not understand why Dymogatsky's play has been banned. When, however, Savva makes it clear that the play's ending is "counterrevolutionary" because it lacks international solidarity between English sailors and red Islanders, who have liberated themselves from capitalist oppression, Gennady and his factotum Metelkin-Passepartout tack on an "international revolution within five minutes."

Although Gennady dominates the play, its central figure on both levels is still Vasily Dymogatsky, who writes under the pen name of Jules Verne and interprets the lead role of Kiri-Kuki in his own comedy. Dymogatsky took months of hard work in a miserable unheated dwelling to write his play while keeping himself alive with hackwriting. The hope of seeing his play on stage encouraged the starving young man, and he collapses when Savva hands down his fatal verdict. It means death for his *Crimson Island,* an end to his creative writing and the return to the privations of everyday life, hopelessness and humiliation. A complete lack of communication between the spheres of existence of Savva as censor and Dymogatsky as playwright gives rise to comic effects amid this human tragedy. For example, Savva mistakes Dymogatsky's desperate lament as part of his role as Kiri-Kuki, and asks him "Where is this from?" Kiri-Dymogatsky replies: "This is from here! From me! From the depths of my heart. . . ."[12] Dymogatsky's grief breaks through both levels of the play to reveal the real drama of an unjustly humiliated writer.

Bulgakov's involvement in theatrical life and his love of dramatic art created in *The Crimson Island* a specific ambiance of theatricality and ambivalence. *The Crimson Island* is sprinkled throughout with unmarked spontaneous quotations from famous plays, according to the actors' tastes. Thus Gennady summons all the actors and declares, in the words of Gogol's Mayor from *The Inspector General,* "I called you in order to tell you. . . ," and then Anempodist Sunduchkov, the future King Sizi-Buzi, finishes the quotation: "the most unpleasant news."[13]

Bulgakov used various means—lights, sounds, and musical effects—to stress his play's main idea. Light effects emphasize the "revolutionary ambience" of the Island's masses; the darkness after the volcanic eruption dissolves when the natives inundate the stage carrying red flags. White Moors change the white feathers of their headdresses to crimson feathers, and their lanterns begin to burn pink instead of white. When Savva arrives, the stage is immediately illuminated with an unnaturally bright red light.

Music, under the direction of the skillful conductor and choir-master Likui Isaich, also plays a role. Thus the British song "Oh, it's a long way to Tipperary" immediately yields to the popular revolutionary song "Warszawianka" (We all come out of common people) to please the censor. At the end of the epilogue, when Dymogatsky-Kiri finally triumphs, he exclaims, like Chekhov's Lopakhin after he had bought the cherry orchard: "I want music!" Overwhelmed with joy, Dymogatsky begins to sing songs which are unsuitable for the occasion, starting with the Russian religious hymn "How glorious is our Lord in Zion" and shifting again to "Oh, it's a long way to Tipperary." Such quick transitions made the performance abundantly entertaining.

The Crimson Island began its short stage life very successfully, but was banned, apparently after no more than four performances, by the combined efforts of hostile critics, one of whom called it "a pitiful spectacle."[14] In March 1929 the play was dropped from the Kamerny Theater repertory. Years later the critic Boris Miliavsky, comparing Bulgakov's play to Mayakovsky's *Bathhouse,* praised Mayakovsky but condemned Bulgakov because Bulgakov "ridicules the very idea of state, Party management of theatrical activities," and because he had directed his play "against any participation of the theater in communist propaganda."[15]

Adam and Eve

Bulgakov wrote *Adam and Eve* at the suggestion of the Leningrad "Red Theater," and in 1931 signed contracts with the Vakhtangov Theater in Moscow for a play on the subject of a future war. It was to be ready by 1 November 1931. However, in the end the Leningrad theater decided it could not produce it.

The play's fate at the Vakhtangov Theater was no better. Bulgakov made some corrections in the text, substituting the more general term "the City" for "Leningrad," and adding a concluding scene in which the entire holocaust of war turned out to be nothing but a hallucination.[16] Bulgakov's concessions turned out to be in vain. To this day *Adam and Eve* has been neither published nor performed in the Soviet Union.[17]

The main theme of the play is the danger of total destruction of life on earth by poison-gas warfare. The destructive power of gas, however, could be neutralized by defensive devices invented by

certain responsible scientists. Two epigraphs elucidate the content
and meaning of the four-act play. One is a passage from a book on
chemical warfare; the other is a fragment from a torn "untitled
book," which is nothing less than a quotation from Genesis, God's
words to Noah after the flood, "neither will I again smite any more
every thing living, as I have done" (8:21). This epigraph and the
title of the play suggest an optimistic view: the holocaust, caused
by men's mutual hatred, will be overcome, and life, preserved by
nature and Adam and Eve, will resume on earth.

The play begins on a May evening as music from the opera *Faust*
fills the first-floor room of the young engineer Adam Krasovsky.
He and his beautiful bride Eve plan to leave the next day for Green
Cape on their honeymoon. Suddenly an absent-minded professor,
Alexander Efrosimov, a famous chemist, jumps in through the window to escape from a drunken baker, Zakhar Markizov, who does
not like "bourgeois parasites" or intellectuals. Efrosimov pretends
to take pictures of Adam and Eve but in fact irradiates them with
his camera, making them immune to lethal gases. The ray also falls
on Ponchik-Nepobeda, a proletarian writer who unexpectedly opens
the door, and on Markizov. Another tenant of the same apartment,
Andrey Daragan, a resolute commander of a fighter squadron, mis-
trusts the pacifist Efrosimov. He calls state security agents and a
psychiatrist: Efrosimov's neutralizing ray belongs to the State De-
fense Committee, and he should have no control over it.

Suddenly total war breaks out: people are poisoned by a "solar"
gas and buildings collapse. Only those irradiated by Efrosimov's ray
survive. They find the dying Daragan, who had been on a combat
mission, and restore him to health with Efrosimov's ray. Adam leads
them all to the woods to save them from plague and starvation in
the infested city. But there is no peace among them, as all the men
compete for Eve's love. Daragan decides to make a reconnaissance
flight, taking Efrosimov's camera with him for self-protection. But
when he also wants to take gas bombs with him, Efrosimov confesses
that he has decomposed the bombs to prevent further destruction.
Daragan thereupon decides to put the scientist on trial for state
treason.

The colonists anxiously wait thirty days for Daragan's return. Eve
declares her love for Efrosimov, her new "Adam," and they decide
to leave the forest colony for an unknown future. Ponchik and
Markizov join them, and Adam, head of the colony, releases every-

one. At that moment Daragan lands with the news that Moscow is only half-destroyed, and people have begun to return in great numbers from the Urals.

In the earlier version, where the city is called Leningrad, the ending is different: Daragan says that he is now "commander of the escort of the Government of the World" and must go to Leningrad. He orders Efrosimov to fly with him, because the Government needs Efrosimov's method of purifying the infected city, promising the scientist freedom afterwards. In the corrected version at the end the lights slowly dim and Adam, Eve, and Efrosimov appear in Adam's room of the first act. All that has happened seems an apocalyptic vision, as Efrosimov protests: "Human fantasy does not have the right to imagine such a thing!" (77). The play ends as it began, with the music of *Faust*.

The play, written, like the earlier story "The Fatal Eggs" in the manner of H. G. Wells, proved to be prophetic, as Soviet citizens began to understand in 1941.[18] Notwithstanding its satirical overtones, this play is Bulgakov's most philosophical and serious dramatic work, for it deals with the most acute problem of our time—how to avert a global war leading to mankind's extermination.[19]

Efrosimov is completely absorbed by this problem. He develops his views on international relations in a conversation with Adam, who believes war is possible because "the capitalist world is filled with hatred" for his socialist country (14). Efrosimov thinks a war is inevitable because the socialist world is also filled with hatred for the capitalist world. The only way to prevent mutual destruction is to neutralize lethal gases and decompose gas bombs. And, Efrosimov says, such "an invention must be given to all countries at once" (18).

Daragan and Adam Krasovsky, both members of the Communist party, realize that Efrosimov's invention can help their government to rule the world, but the war intervenes. The discussion of war resumes among the six survivors in the forest. Daragan and Adam are capable of thinking only in standard Soviet terms, and consider Efrosimov a traitor. The two comic figures—the alcoholic baker Markizov and the opportunist writer Ponchik—display much more human understanding than Daragan and Adam. Markizov prevented Daragan from shooting Efrosimov outright, while Ponchik disrupted the "trial" whose preordained verdict was death to Efrosimov (57–58, 61). Bulgakov ridicules Ponchik's "ideologically correct" novel about some "starving peasants" working for a count who, after the Revolution, were replaced in the fields by red-cheeked, happy collective farm girls. When he finds himself alone in the ruined city, Ponchik begins to pray, confessing to God that he worked for the journal the *Atheist* solely out of thoughtlessness (39). Later, in the forest, rebelling against Adam's dictatorship, Ponchik regrets that he had written "a groveling novel" (69). However, as soon as Ponchik learns the previous way of life is being restored, he regrets that he has destroyed his novel. Markizov rightly calls him a real "snake."

Markizov reads a scrap of the Bible about Adam and Eve before they were seduced by the serpent. Eve chooses Efrosimov as her real "Adam" because she loves nature, peace, the quiet life, and individual people, and rejects Adam Krasovsky's projects for building socialist society with "human material" instead of individual human beings (71).

Bliss and *Ivan Vasil'evich*

The central device of the plays *Bliss* and *Ivan Vasil'evich* is a time machine that makes it possible for man to transcend time and space. However, this scientific achievement collides with the trivialities of everyday life and difficulties in communication between people of different historical periods and views. *Bliss* was completed in 1934 but was neither produced nor published during Bulgakov's lifetime.

Subtitled "The Dream of Engineer Rein," *Bliss* depicts Rein working on his apparatus in the typical setting of a Moscow communal apartment in the early 1930s. The usual nasty personage— the house manager Bunsha-Koretsky—controls the life of his tenants and constantly disrupts Rein's activities. [20] The time machine finally begins to work, whisking Rein and Bunsha into the epoch of the Czar Ivan the Terrible. Rein manages to switch the machine off and to return to his room, but the wall separating his room from that of his neighbor Michelson collapses and the thief Yury Miloslavsky appears. Now all three—Miloslavsky, Bunsha, and Rein—are transported to the twenty-third century, the year 2222, and a perfectly rational and harmonious socialist society.

Radamanov, the People's commissar for invention, and his daughter Avrora are at first astonished by the appearance of three strange men at their glass tower in the Bliss district of Moscow, but later they welcome their visitors. Avrora falls in love with Rein and rejects a proposal from Ferdinand Savvich, director of the Institute of Harmony. Miloslavsky, while pretending to be a poet, robs high officials and courts Radamanov's secretary Anna.

Bunsha spies upon Rein and Avrora and denounces them to Savvich, who declares all three twentieth-century visitors dangerous to the new society. The administration of his Institute resolves to imprison them in a psychiatric clinic. Radamanov, a seemingly understanding person, confiscates Rein's machine. At Avrora's suggestion Rein decides to escape. Miloslavsky picks the lock of the state safe where the time machine has been taken, and they all return to Rein's room in Moscow, bringing Avrora with them. The police, who are there investigating the theft from Michelson's room, arrest Bunsha, Rein, and Avrora. Miloslavsky escapes through the window in a flying machine he has stolen from the Bliss safe. Michelson, to whom Miloslavsky has returned all his stolen possessions, concludes the play with the words: "That, comrades, is what happened in our Bathhouse Lane. But if I tell it at the office or to my friends, no one will believe it, no one!" (107).

The comedy abounds in humorous situations and ambiguous controversies. For example, Bulgakov satirizes the official belief that life in socialist society will always improve. Even the twenty-third-century functionary Radamanov disagrees with Savvich that in the twenty-sixth century life will be better than in their time. As in Evgeny Zamyatin's future society in his novel *We,* the activities of Bliss inhabitants are controlled by the Council of People's Commissars of the World and the Institute of Harmony. After his conversation with Radamanov in act 3, Rein realizes that if he does not give his time machine to the People's Commissariat of Inventions, he will die. But even after he submits to Radamanov's pressures, Savvich incarcerates him and his fellow travelers. Avrora is bored with the programmed existence of Bliss society, and seeks only to escape.

Yury Miloslavsky,[21] a virtuoso thief and adventurer, recalls certain characters from Bulgakov's earlier works. He is understandably bored in the twenty-third century's regulated society, where he cannot display any initiative. And Bunsha, an opportunist who adjusts to the Soviet system by concealing his "social origins," is a typical personage of Bulgakov's stories. He spies on everybody, denouncing "suspicious" tenants of the house he controls. Bunsha does not understand how the inhabitants of Bliss can live without trade union identification, without food ration cards or police registrations. He feels lost without his bureaucratic duties to perform.

The central character, Eugene Rein, is a talented scientist who devotes himself entirely to his invention. When the time machine brings Ivan the Terrible to contemporary Moscow, the sixteenth-century tyrant is terrified by the sight of twentieth-century Soviet citizens: he takes them for devils and tries to ward them off by making the sign of the cross (80). But before the czar can be seized by the police, Rein succeeds in sending Ivan back to his own time. Avrora's fate is much sadder. Her love for Rein and her naive belief that she will find happiness with him in his own time result in the immediate arrest of both of them. We do not know what happens to them.

It is obvious that in the 1930s a satire with such strong political overtones would frighten the director of the Leningrad Music Hall, who intended to produce *Bliss*. In a letter of July 1934, Bulgakov described his meeting with the Music Hall director as a fantastic episode. The director listened with obvious delight to Bulgakov's reading of his play, said he wanted to perform it, and invited Bulgakov for dinner. At the dinner he said not a word about the play, and never offered Bulgakov a contract. [22] Then Bulgakov signed a contract for *Bliss* with the Moscow Theater of Satire. However, before long substantial revisions were required, and by a new contract of October 1934 Bulgakov agreed to rework his play. The new version became *Ivan Vasil'evich*. [23]

Although there are similar scenes in *Bliss* and *Ivan Vasil'evich*, especially at the beginning and the end, the two plays are different. *Bliss*'s futurological philosophy and science fiction features vanished with the dropping of the flight into the future. Now the main action involves "piercing time" into the past. The ballad "Prince Mikhailo Repnin" by Alexey K. Tolstoy (written in the 1840s, published in 1867), which Miloslavsky recites, serves as a leitmotiv of Ivan the Terrible. Hoarse, distorted sounds from Rimsky-Korsakov's opera *A Woman from Pskov* (1872–92), in which Czar Ivan is the central figure, serve the same purpose.

The main character is the same devoted, idealistic scientist, though now his name is Nikolay Timofeev and he works on a huge apparatus that resembles a radio. He is disturbed in his work by raucous music from a faulty radio but falls asleep in exhaustion. Now reality and fantasy are so closely interlaced that sometimes their borders blur. Timofeev's wife Zina, an actress, tells him that his striving to capture past and future is utopian. In his dream Timofeev sees her running away with a movie producer Yakin, whose very existence Zina denies at the end of the play.

The thief George Miloslavsky, in the course of robbing Timofeev's neighbor Anton Shpak, recites a monologue similar to Yury Miloslavsky's from *Bliss*. The unpleasant house manager Bunsha-Koretsky, whose name is now Ivan Vasil'evich, like the czar's, bears a striking physical resemblance to Ivan the Terrible. Through Timofeev's time machine Bunsha and Miloslavsky are thrown back into the sixteenth-century czar's palace, while the historical Ivan the Terrible appears in Timofeev's Moscow communal apartment and talks to him. The fantastic illusion is shattered by Shpak's desperate shouting for the police when he discovers the theft of his possessions.

All sorts of humorous situations result when three such personages are transferred to another time. In his dream, Timofeev sees the denouement—the return of each character to his own time, the destruction of the time machine by the angry czar, and the arrival of the police, who arrest Timofeev, Bunsha, and Miloslavsky. The sounds of the Rimsky-Korsakov opera awaken Timofeev; his wife Zina enters the room, and Shpak runs in yelling that he has been robbed in reality, and not just in Timofeev's fantastic dream.

For all its lighthearted playfulness, this comedy poses the interesting problem of how people of different epochs would communicate, how they would behave in completely unfamiliar circumstances. Czar Ivan does not lose his dignity—even in the strange environment of the twentieth century, he is still very much czar. For example, he worries about the seizure of a particular area by the Swedish army: state interests of this time need his presence.

In the third act, we see only the rascal Miloslavsky is able to adjust partly to sixteenth-century conditions: he pretends to be the czar's "favorite" and adviser, befriends the deacon Fedor, and gives absurd orders to the czar's special guard. The narrow-minded Bunsha continues to look at everything with his house managerial "unslumbering eye." And as soon as he returns to his own time, he denounces Timofeev: "I confess I was a czar, but only as a result of Engineer Timofeev's infamous experiment" (471).

The Theater of Satire was ready to perform *Ivan Vasil'evich* in May 1936, but it was banned at the last moment. The comedy was first performed with great success only much later, in 1965, in Moscow.[24] Both comedies were later performed in Paris by Russian actors— *Ivan Vasil'evich* in 1971, and *Bliss* in 1978.[25]

Chapter Six

Bulgakov's "Molièriana"

Bulgakov's "Molièriana" consists of a free adaptation of Molière's plays entitled *Poloumnyi Zhurden (Half-Witted Jourdain)*, the play *Kabala sviatosh (A Cabal of Hypocrites)* or *Molière*, and the biographical novel *The Life of Monsieur de Molière*. Bulgakov turned to Molière in the late 1920s, when he had been ostracized by the Moscow literary and artistic world.

Bulgakov's first comments on Molière date from October 1929, and his addiction to Molière lasted many years, when, as he put it himself, he "lived in the illusive and fantastic seventeenth-century Paris."

Bulgakov discovered in Molière's art the grotesque carnival spirit that was close to his own art. His interest in Molière was motivated not only by his desire to gain deeper insight into Molière's brilliant stage techniques and characterizations, but also by a need to find in Molière's life certain parallels with his own plight. Bulgakov's experience with Moscow backstage life for five years brought Molière's problems close to his heart, for then he realized that "it was impossible to write plays without being able to produce them."[1] Molière became for Bulgakov a symbol of the perennial force of true Art.

Half-Witted Jourdain

In 1932 the Moscow Theater-Studio, headed by Yury Zavadsky, asked Bulgakov to translate *Le Bourgeois gentilhomme*, written by Molière in the summer of 1670 at the command of King Louis XIV, in collaboration with the composer Jean-Baptiste Lully, and with the advice of Laurent D'Arvieux, a specialist on Turkish language and customs.

Bulgakov signed a contract with the Theater-Studio in July 1932 and devoted three months to an intensive study of several Molière's plays. On 18 November 1932, he delivered the play *Half-Witted Jourdain*, subtitled "Molièriana in Three Acts." It was not accepted for production. What Bulgakov had written was variations on themes from Molière's plays, with a vivid re-creation, in the first scene of the first act, of the real process of staging a theatrical performance, as presented in Molière's one-act comedy *L'Impromptu de Versailles*.

Bulgakov's interest in the daily life of Molière's troupe is convincingly manifested by this first scene adjusted chronologically: from Versailles of 1663 the action was transferred to the king's castle at Chambord in 1670. The original list of the actors participating in the 1663 performance of *L'Impromptu de Versailles* was also adjusted to correspond to the list of the actors premiering *Le Bourgeois gentilhomme* in 1670. For instance, Hubert, an actor of the Marais Theater, joined Molière's troupe in 1664, and specialized in playing old women. Accordingly, he appears as Mme Jourdain in Bulgakov's play. In March 1667 the celebrated actress and dancer Thérèse Marquise Du Parc left Molière after fourteen years of collaboration and transferred to the Theater Hôtel de Bourgogne with a friend, the young playwright Jean Racine, and her name vanished from Bulgakov's list. Louis Béjart, who retired in April of 1670 after twenty-five years of close collaboration with Molière, was introduced into Bulgakov's play as the only person able to substitute for the sick Molière. Indeed, since 1665 Molière's health had deteriorated, and his doctors were of little help. These changes in the original 1663 cast of characters demonstrate the meticulous attention Bulgakov paid to historical fact in his attempt to reconstruct the activities of Molière's troupe. Brindavoine is the only fictitious name Bulgakov gave to Molière's servant, who also acts as the servant of Mr. Jourdain.[2]

Half-Witted Jourdain begins with the appearance of Louis Béjart, who, tired after a long day's work, wants to rush to a little tavern where his friends and a glass of wine await him. His dream is disturbed by Brindavoine, who gives him a letter from Molière, the director, who is sick, and asks Béjart to substitute for him in rehearsing for the next day's performance at Chambord. Béjart summarizes for the actors in one sentence ths subject of the new comedy, and announces that he has had to replace Molière in the part of Jourdain, a rich Paris bourgeois who goes mad pretending that he is a nobleman. Béjart briefly explains to each actor the essential features of his part. Immediately the stage is transformed into Jourdain's splendid living room, and the play within a play begins.

Bulgakov made several cuts in *Le Bourgeois gentilhomme* and added scenes taken from other plays of his. Thus, Bulgakov modeled a conversation between the Master of Music and the Master of Dance on some scenes from Molière's first and second acts. The scene with the Master of Arms quarreling with other Masters ends with his expulsion and with Jourdain's request to see some beautiful theatrical scenes to feel the potential beauty of the prose that was explained to him by Pancrace, the Master of Philosophy: Pancrace figures in the comedy *Le Mariage forcé* (1664). Bulgakov also introduced the concluding scene of *Don Juan,* which the Master of Music staged to entertain Mr. Jourdain. Suddenly Mme Jourdain appears from nowhere and drives the Statue and Don Juan out of her house.[3]

In his third act Bulgakov used the "Turkish" masquerade of Molière's acts 3 and 4. Finally everyone, including Mme Jourdain and her daughter Lucile, are involved in the carnivalesque comedy, and all understand what is going on except Mr. Jourdain, who is still blinded by his own illusions. Even the presence of a lawyer, who drew up three marriage contracts, does not help Mr. Jourdain to distinguish between reality—the marriage of the servants Covielle and Nicole—and the carnivalesque marriage of the "Turkish sultan," a disguised Cléonte, to his daughter Lucile. While there is no actual denouement in Molière's comedy, which he ended with songs and the "ballet of the three nations," Bulgakov added Cléonte's realistic explanation of what had just been achieved by unmasking all the participants. Bulgakov's Jourdain, refusing to accept facts, asks Pancrace, his teacher of philosophy, to comfort him with "something agreeable." "With pleasure," answers Pancrace: "The performance is finished."[4]

After these words Béjart removes his Turkish clothes, puts on his black cape, takes a lantern, and announces that "Everyone is free." To the music of a march, Béjart finally escapes the day's troubles; he hurries to the tavern and invites the audience to join him there. In this way the play within a play was ended and the connections with Molière's life and activities established, though the great playwright himself did not appear on the stage.

A Cabal of Hypocrites or *Molière*

The play *A Cabal of Hypocrites,* later renamed *Molière* (1929–30), presents variations on Molière's life by focusing on certain dramatic events which led to his premature death. Unfortunately, we lack space here for a detailed comparison of this complex play with the facts of Molière's life, so we will concentrate on the play itself.

A *Cabal of Hypocrites* is an ingenious, original work in which Bulgakov introduced historically authentic persons as well as fictitious characters based on real prototypes. His intent in this play was to present on stage the torment of a genius whose best works were misinterpreted and banned, and who was accused of being a pernicious corruptor of society. Therefore Bulgakov did not show Molière at the peak of his career, but rather a persecuted Molière, who, nevertheless, did not succumb to his various foes.

In his four-act play Bulgakov disregards the classical unities. The action takes place on the stage of the Palais Royal Theater in Paris, in two dressing rooms, one belonging to Molière and the other to La Grange, where La Grange writes his "Register"; in the sumptuous reception room of the king; in Molière's apartment; in a stone cellar where the members of the Company of the Holy Writ meet secretly; in a confessional of the cathedral; and, finally, once more in Molière's home and on the stage. Thus there is no unity of place, nor of time, for the action in the play shifts from one crucial episode of Molière's life to another.

Bulgakov's play begins at the time Molière's troupe was performing under the name of "Comédiens de Monsieur" (or "La Compagnie de Monsieur") under the protection of Duke Philippe d'Orléans, only brother of King Louis XIV. In act 1, showing a spectacle at the Palais Royal Theater, the stage represents two dressing rooms. La Grange is alone in his dressing room, where he keeps the chronicles of Molière's life and of the performance of his plays. Molière is very excited because Louis XIV has honored his troupe by his presence for the first time.

After the performance, Molière informs Madelaine, his loyal companion and former mistress, of his decision to marry Armande, whom he believed to be Madelaine's younger sister. The young Moirron, in concealment, overhears the intimacies of a love scene between Molière and Armande as well as a private conversation between La Grange and Madelaine. Moirron learns the secrets behind the glorious facade of the actors' life and in particular that Armande is Madelaine's daughter and not her sister, as everybody believes. When Molière discovers Moirron, he takes him to his house.

Several years elapse between the first and the second acts. Act 2 shows the king's courtiers plotting against Molière. Archbishop Charron asks the king to listen to a vagrant preacher, Father Barthélemy, who accuses Molière of being the Anti-Christ, and demands that he be burned. But no one can *demand* that King Louis XIV do anything: the insolent Father Barthélemy is immediately incarcerated. The king believes that Molière can magnify the glory of his reign with his talent as well as amuse the court, and allows him to stage *Tartuffe* at the Palais Royal.

The scene changes to Molière's house, where Moirron, now a brilliant and handsome actor of twenty-three, is courting Armande, as they play in real life their roles as lovers from Molière's tragedy-ballet *Psyché*. Molière drives Moirron from his house, and the enraged youth threatens to expose Molière's "secret" to the king.

Act 3 deals with the actions taken by the members of the Company of the Holy Writ against Molière. Archbishop Charron, the most influential person at court, is present at a meeting of the Company and interrogates Moirron for the purpose of uncovering more compromising evidence against Molière.

In the next scene, at the cathedral, Madelaine Béjart confesses her sins to Archbishop Charron, who threatens her with eternal damnation and learns that Armande is indeed her daughter. Using this information in the next scene, in the reception room of the king, Charron adds accusations of a sinful private life to the already known instances of Molière's impiety as manifested in *Tartuffe* and *Don Juan*. The king, though disgusted with Moirron's denunciation of Molière, cannot risk countenancing an "offense against religion." The king tells Molière that he is forbidden to stage *Tartuffe*, and is deprived of the royal patronage.

In act 4 the settings are changed twice. Molière is in his apartment with his servant Bouton and La Grange. Armande, his wife, has deserted him, and his favorite disciple, Moirron, has betrayed him. Molière says to La Grange, "It is Fate which has come to my house and stolen everything from me."[5] Moirron appears and kneels before Molière, saying he no longer deserves to live, and Molière forgives him. Though sick, Molière insists on acting in his new comedy *Le Malade Imaginaire (Imaginary Invalid)*, and dies on stage of a heart attack.

The Marquis de Charron, archbishop of Paris, modeled upon a historical figure, the archbishop of Paris, Cardinal Hardouin de

Beaumont de Péréfixe, embodies all the forces opposed to Molière and his work. One of his instruments is the Company, which condemns the theater for propagating freethinking, and in particular seeks a ban on *Tartuffe*.

In his play Bulgakov focused attention on two major issues: Molière's efforts to secure the king's patronage, and to restage *Tartuffe*, banned after its premiere in 1664. Though historically some events in Bulgakov's play do not conform to the facts, it is also true that Molière was losing ground with the king, and he knew moments of despair, confusion, and hopelessness.

Molière's monologue in act 4 of Bulgakov's play is a most significant expression of a great man's moral defeat in his struggle against a despotic power. Molière hypocritically humiliated himself in order to please the king; he was always aware that if he lost the king's favor, he would perish as an artist and theater director. Now Molière fears Louis the Great, "the Golden idol with cold green eyes," and cannot free himself from his power: "All my life I licked his spurs, and I kept thinking just one thing: don't crush me. And now he is crushing me anyway. The tyrant!"[6]

Indeed, Molière never missed an occasion to flatter the king and frequently debased himself in order to save his works, especially *Tartuffe*. With this play banned, all his efforts seemed in vain, and then he rebelled against "the king's tyranny." Nevertheless, though Molière was sick and frightened, he still cherished his vocation. The theater constituted his whole life; its artificial world provided him freedom to challenge men and society while exposing their vices and defects. He could not miss the performances of his final comedy *Le Malade Imaginaire*. As Bulgakov's play ends, La Grange writes the saddest page of his *Register:* "February seventeenth. It was the fourth performance of the play *Le Malade Imaginaire*, written by Monsieur de Molière. At ten o'clock in the evening Monsieur de Molière, playing the role of Argan, fell down on the stage and was seized on the spot, without confession, by inexorable death."[7]

In reality La Grange noted that death was caused by a ruptured artery, while in Bulgakov's play La Grange suggested that the prime cause of death was "the disfavor of the king and the black Cabal!"

The Novel *Life of Monsieur de Molière*

The play *A Cabal of Hypocrites* and the novel *Life of Monsieur de Molière* are very closely connected: the Soviet theater specialist Konstantin Rudnitsky has called the latter an "Introduction" to the former.[8] Indeed, Bulgakov's novel brings the reader closer to Molière's world, the clash between him and the contemporary authorities.

Bulgakov's novel, written in 1932–33, is not a traditional academic work done within the limited framework of a documentary study. Neither is it a chronological analysis of Molière's plays with a few notes on his life. It is rather a romanticized life story, in which Bulgakov wanted to re-create the real Molière, man, artist, and playwright, living the everyday life of the seventeenth century, a life full of conflict, trouble, and suffering. Bulgakov stayed quite close to the historical facts as known in the late 1920s, but he interpreted them creatively for his own purposes.

The novel consists of thirty-three chapters with prologue and epilogue. Bulgakov uses his typical chapter headings, such as "Not Everybody Likes to Be an Upholsterer," "Look out, Bourgogne— Molière Is Coming!," or "May Lightning Strike Molière." Bulgakov frequently refers to La Grange and his Register, with records of the performances of Molière's plays starting in 1659, and it appears certain that Bulgakov knew Grimarest's early biography of Molière, *La Vie de Mr. de Molière.*[9] Apparently Bulgakov took his title from the Grimarest book in order to suggest that he was writing as a contemporary of Molière's.

To realize his creative intent, Bulgakov employs a complex system of narrative voices: he will act as a narrator-witness, but also, invisibly, he will be present as the author himself, an empathetic author who mirrors his own personality, interrupting from time to time with his own observations.

Bulgakov plays the role of Molière's contemporary, but one who already knows the future and thus can evaluate certain facts and episodes of Molière's life from an enlightened perspective. The narrator thus allows his readers to grasp the future in the present and past. For example, while relating the events of 1659, the narrator mentions a young man named Charles Varlet de La Grange whom Molière liked and accepted into his troupe. The narrator comments: "And, in the view of those who have studied the life of my hero for several centuries, this was a most fortunate action,"[10] for, without his famous Register, as the narrator says, "we would know still less about our hero than we know today, or, to put it more precisely, we would know virtually nothing."

Bulgakov's narrator accompanies Molière through critical episodes of his life, and then, like a second La Grange, hastens to record them. The narrator is obviously present from the very first line of the prologue "I speak to a Midwife" to the last line of the epilogue, when he takes leave of his hero. The narrator does not wear any mask, but does adopt certain devices. Thus, in order to speak to the midwife who attended Madame Poquelin at the birth of her first child, he blends into the seventeenth-century environment by donning a caftan with huge pockets and telling the midwife how important for France is the fragile baby whom she cradles in her arms: his fame will even reach distant Muscovy.

The narrator begins a friendly talk with his readers by a description of the Poquelin family. Before long the narrative takes the form of a fine theatrical scene: as the narrator sits in a chair, the door opens, and one by one the personages of Molière's life come on stage: "And now, by the light of my candle, I see a gentleman of bourgeois appearance. . . . His name is Louis, his surname Cressé" (20).

There follows a vivid description of the theatrical presentations that the young Jean-Baptiste and his grandfather Louis Cressé see at the Pont Neuf. The narrator imagines that the plots of Molière's future comedies formed in his mind at that time. When Jean-Baptiste expresses a wish to study, the narrator declines to repeat the conversation which took place between the boy's father and his grandfather, who supported the boy's wish: "I shall merely exclaim: Oh, Louis Cressé of hallowed memory!" (31).

Touching again on the controversial subject of Molière's love for Armande, the narrator, seeing Molière hurrying from the theater to visit Madelaine's sixteen-year-old sister, asks: "Are you sure that she is Madelaine's sister? . . . He does not want to answer. It may well be that he does not know. Why, then, waste words on the subject? . . ." (105). Still, the narrator devotes the eighteenth chapter, entitled "Who Is She?," to Molière's wedding on 20 February 1662. After reviewing all the available documents, the narrator first seems to ask his readers' opinion on the subject, but then concludes "that Armande was Madelaine's daughter, that her birth was secret, in an unknown place, and by an unknown father" (138). The most important fact was that the mature Armande did not respond to the love of her ailing husband.

In observing the young Molière, the narrator noted that he was subject to abrupt changes of mood, and added "that with these characteristics he will not have an easy life, and will make many enemies" (40). This image of Molière as a sensitive, quick-tempered man who was deeply hurt by the attacks of critics, foes, and other envious people, is a central one. Unfortunately, he was subjected to slanderous assaults from the beginning to the end, but avenged himself by creating immortal farcical figures of them.

Bulgakov's main purpose was to trace Molière's artistic development and to reveal the great effort also required to find talented actors, obtain suitable theater halls, and most especially to procure a powerful patron. Indeed, Molière knew too well the value of adequate patronage for the very existence of his troupe.[11] In August 1665 he was permitted to name his troupe "La Troupe du Roi au Palais Royal," which rescued him from the ruin sought by the Cabal, but also placed him under heavy obligation to the king.

Along with the privilege of being in the special service of his majesty, Molière now had to write and produce magnificent shows because the king liked dance, music, songs, and sumptuous settings. Thus, several comedy-ballets were added to the long list of royal diversions, and two of them were written at the king's request. While staging these entertainment pieces, Molière also vented his creative genius in satirizing men's vices and psychological and mental defects. To this end he created *Le Misanthrope*, *L'Avare (The Miser)*, *Le Malade Imaginaire (The Imaginary Invalid)*, and *Les Femmes Savantes (The Learned Ladies)*, as the narrator comments, "not to order, but for himself" (205).

Bulgakov's narrator reviews the controversy over *Tartuffe*, which was denounced as "abominable."[12] The narrator is especially interested in Molière's conduct after the banning of *Tartuffe:* "And what did the author of the luckless play do?," he asks. "Did he burn it? Or hide it? No. As soon as he recovered from the Versailles scandal, the unrepentant playwright sat down to write the fourth and fifth acts of *Tartuffe*" (158). This statement, of course, also refers to another "unrepentant playwright"—Bulgakov himself. Both narrative voices contribute to a sympathetic description of Molière's attempts to revive *Tartuffe* by reducing it and presenting it under the title *The Imposter* in 1667: "He has resurrected his Lazarus, but the latter lived only one evening of 5 August" (179), for it was immediately banned again.

Suddenly, in early 1669, in spite of all previous prohibitions, *Tartuffe the Imposter* was staged again. Bulgakov's narrator poses the question: "Who can illuminate the tortuous paths of a comedian's life? Who will explain to me why a play that could not be performed in 1664 and 1667 could be performed in 1669?" (185).

Again, we hear the second narrative voice: why was *The Days of the Turbins* barred with such an uproar in 1929, and then allowed to be performed in 1932?

Many details of Molière's last day, as related by Bulgakov's narrator, correspond to the description given by La Grange and Grimarest of the day of the fourth and final performance of *Le Malade Imaginaire*. The narrator, noting that it was also the anniversary of Madelaine's death, comments that in this play "Molière mocked the most irrational fear existing among men, the fear of death and obsessive preoccupation with health" (208). Indeed, *Le Malade Imaginaire* contains a heroic attempt to overcome the anguish of serious illness and the menace of death by satirizing any extreme preoccupation with it. In Molière's comedy Argan asks whether it is not dangerous to imitate death, as if this were a bad omen. As J. D. Hubert has explained, "After all, his imaginary death might suddenly become as real as his imaginary disease!"[13] During the fourth performance of the play, these words suddenly acquired tragic meaning. Molière lay on the stage in the guise of a grotesque personage, true almost to his last breath to his pure passion for the theater and dramatic art.

Bulgakov terminates the story of Molière's life by evoking the image of the "Fontaine de Molière" monument, which he mentioned in the prologue.[14] For Bulgakov, this is the apotheosis of the playwright's genius. Molière's papers and manuscripts were destroyed, the site of his grave lost, but something remained: "One day, though robbed of both his manuscripts and letters, he left the plot of earth he had shared with suicides and stillborn infants and took up his place over the basin of a dried-out fountain." At the end of his book Bulgakov restores the unity of both narrative voices: "There he is! It is he, the king's comedian, with bronze bows on his shoes. And I, who am never to see him, send him my farewell greetings" (224).

Clearly, Bulgakov saw Molière as the embodiment of his own ideals, trials, and concerns, as, in short, his favorite "hero." Bulgakov appeared to have almost relived Molière's life, perceiving the tragedy beneath laughter and buffoonery of Molière's comedies and farces. Bulgakov decoded the statements of Molière's protagonists in which bitter truth was veiled under burlesque masks, separating out the true voice of the suffering playwright.

Bulgakov refused to rewrite his novel to eliminate the narrator, as the editors of the Biographical Series demanded. By this act of courage and despair he preserved his image of Molière and saved his work, which appeared only in 1962, but in its original form.[15]

Chapter Seven
The "Sunset" Novel

Bulgakov began *The Master and Margarita* in 1928, and though he destroyed the first version in 1930, it occupied his mind until the very last moments of his life. While working on his semi-autobiographical *Theatrical Novel*, Bulgakov returned for the fourth time to "the novel on the devil" which had been finally designated *The Master and Margarita* since September 1937. Bulgakov's archives preserve eight versions of the novel which took twenty-six years to be published. There now exist two published versions of the novel, both of which have been translated into English.

A detailed study of all the manuscript versions of the work, designated under different titles—beginning with a general description as "a novel on the devil," later under more specific titles such as "A Black Magician," "The Hoof of the Engineer," "The Consultant with a Hoof"—has been published by the Soviet researcher Marietta Chudakova.[1] As several phases of Bulgakov's work on this novel have already been described in the first chapter of this book, in this chapter we shall analyze the novel as a completed work of art.

In *The Master and Margarita* Bulgakov gave free rein to fantasy combined with observation of real life and metaphysical meditations. The result is a multileveled work in which realistic, satirical, fantastic, and mystical elements are closely intertwined. Bulgakov complicated its structure by interweaving into the pluralistic description of twentieth-century Moscow reality an action that had occurred centuries earlier.

The novel tells of events that occur in Moscow during four days beginning on a Wednesday evening and ending on a Saturday night in May, with the Master and Margarita finding their eternal peaceful refuge. It has two parts with thirty-two chapters and an epilogue. Each chapter has an ironic, dramatic, comic, or metaphoric title. The "truthful narrator," as he calls himself, observes everything and invites the reader to follow him. To be sure, the tone of the narration changes according to the meaning of the episodes depicted, which has prompted a few scholars to speak of several different narrators.[2] The most disparate elements are not given separately but are outwardly and inwardly closely connected and constantly intermingled.

In the middle of Moscow of the 1930s, on a hot May day, two Soviet literati are relaxing at Patriarchs' Ponds. An influential functionary, Mikhail Alexandrovich Berlioz, chairman of the board of the Moscow Literary Association, and a young poet, Ivan Ponyrev—known by his pen name, Bezdomny (Homeless)—discuss Ivan's poem on Christ. Suddenly a stranger, a foreign professor named Voland, a specialist in black magic, interrupts their discussion. To convince them that Christ really existed, he tells them the story of Yeshua Hah-Notsri, who was executed by Pilate. The stranger also insists that the devil exists too. The stranger's prediction that Berlioz's life is in danger comes true immediately when he falls under a streetcar and is decapitated. Ivan pursues the stranger, whom he takes for a foreign spy, to the famous Griboedov House, a writers' center, where he is arrested and taken to a psychiatric clinic.

The next day all kinds of diabolical tricks befall Moscow residents. Stepa Likhodeev, director of the Variety Theater, mysteriously disappears from his apartment, which is immediately occupied by Voland and his team; Nikanor Bosoi, the house committee chairman, is bribed by Voland's aide Koroviev-Fagot, while the rubles he gives to Nikanor become dollars. Other tricks occur at the Variety Theater: an evening of black magic staged by Koroviev-Fagot and a huge black cat ends with a scandal.

In the meantime Ivan is visited by a patient from the neighboring ward, a Master, who informs him that Ivan has fallen victim to Satan. The Master tells Ivan of his secret love for a beautiful woman, and of his novel about Yeshua and Pontius Pilate. But venomous critics have destroyed his life, and in a moment of depression he threw his novel into the fire. After the Master has told him his story, Ivan dreams of Yeshua's execution.

The Master's secret love—Margarita—does not forget her beloved. To learn about his fate, she bargains with the devil Azazello, and becomes a witch. She presides over Voland's satanic ball and is rewarded by a meeting with the Master, whose novel magically arises from the ashes. The lovers are returned to the Master's little apartment; there, before they are poisoned by Azazello, Margarita rereads the last two chapters of the Master's novel about the events that had occurred in Yershalaim that Friday night. After their death, on Saturday evening, the Master and Margarita leave Moscow together with Voland and his gang. They are taken to their last peaceful refuge, but beforehand the Master releases his hero, Pontius Pilate, who tries to join Yeshua. In the epilogue, only one person—the former poet Ivan, now a professor of history—remembers the story of Pilate and the Master.

The novel is pervaded with a generally mysterious atmosphere, where the most unbelievable events prove to be realistic, while the seemingly most realistic facts turn out to be phantasmagoric. Multiple layers of meaning lead to ambiguities that leave ample room for the reader's imagination.

Among the interwoven parallel plotlines we may distinguish four: (1) the portrayal of contemporary Moscow reality in a satirical tone; (2) the intrusion of Voland and his gang into Moscow life, which creates a mystico-phantasmagorical world, a kind of grotesque carnival that also serves to unify the intricate narrative; (3) the drama of the Master, a writer who cannot publish his work, and of his love for Margarita; (4) the story of Yeshua's tragedy and Pilate's sin, where a sudden change of style and elaborate vocabulary stress the utmost importance of the events which occurred two thousand years ago in Yershalaim. In developing the first and third plotlines, Bulgakov uses his own experience, but the second and fourth demanded extensive study of historical and biblical sources as well as a scrutiny of demonology and mythology.

Contemporary Moscow

The first important reality in the novel is the city itself. No other work of modern literature presents such a vivid picture of Moscow in the spring; Bulgakov's descriptions of the city's places vividly evoke the old, vanishing Moscow. Bulgakov placed many important events in the "Griboedov House," a cover name for the "Herzen House," where in the early 1920s the Literary Institute had been installed. At the end of the novel the city appears again in all the fairy-tale beauty of its gingerbread palace towers, monasteries, and church domes.[3]

All kinds of events occur in this city: pure love, genuine inspiration, and first-class scientific activity coexist with the most banal and dishonest aspects of life. It should be noted, though, that the description of Moscow mixes elements typical of the 1920s with facts from the life of the 1930s.

In the four days of the narration the narrator opens the doors of
Moscow houses and shows that Moscow inhabitants have not changed
their habits: they are still as interested as ever in good food, housing,
fashionable clothes, entertainment, and money. "The black magic"
helps to uncover the faults and vices of modern Moscovites. They
are tested by Voland, whose main purpose in visiting Moscow is to
see its inhabitants "en masse," as he says to the bartender Sokov
(624), and to discover whether the people of Moscow had changed
"outwardly" and, especially, "inwardly" (537–38). This "vital question," as Koroviev-Fagot calls it, is answered in the negative. Not
only do the former faults of human nature persist, they are aggravated by new defects caused by shortages of almost everything.

Examples of this include a modest bartender who accumulates
several hundred thousand rubles, Nikanor Bosoi (Barefooted), chairman of a house on Sadovaya Street, who takes bribes; and many
others. To stress the diabolic essence of denunciations, a widespread
and vile phenomenon of the 1930s, the author has Koroviev denounce Nikanor after having given him as bribes 400 rubles which
turned into dollars. Koroviev also denounces the tenant Kvasov,
who was spying on Nikanor to denounce him, and the Master is
denounced by his false friend Aloisius Mogarych, who wants to
obtain the Master's modest apartment.

Also characteristic of this period were the arrests of people who
had committed no crime. Such events are so abnormal and irrational
that they could only result from a diabolic force, and the narrator
reports them as some kind of grotesque farce. One apartment, which
belonged to Mme Fougeret, became "haunted" long before the intrusion of Voland and his demons. One after another the tenants
are called out of their rooms by a policeman for a short talk and
never return. The old maid Anfisa ascribes their disappearance to
devilry, and the narrator remarks that "Witchcraft once started, as
is well known, is virtually unstoppable" (492). That proves correct
when Anfisa herself and Mme Fougeret both vanish. Nikanor Bosoi
undergoes a nightmarish interrogation and prison confinement with
hundreds of other people accused of illegally possessing gold and
foreign currency. Investigations, apartment searches, interrogations,
arrests—the facts of a gloomy reality are presented in the novel as
a grotesque dream of a diabolic theatrical performance.

This Moscow reality contains, as in the *Theatrical Novel,* both
humorous parody and bitter satire on the new literary men of the

day. Bulgakov's contemporaries easily recognized the situation when the Russian Association of Proletarian Writers headed by Leopold Averbakh (pictured in the novel under the name of Ahriman) organized a veritable "witchhunt" against writers of independent mind.

Bulgakov satirized the banality and pettiness of the "new" writers' interests in grotesque scenes at the Griboedov House. The members of Griboedov House are no longer writers: they are "members of the MASSOLIT," the monstrous name of the association from which they try to get better apartments, *dachas,* and other privileges.

The poet Ivan Bezdomny, author of poor verses and an antireligious poem, which, however, was not antireligious enough for his editors, repudiates this pseudoliterary world and after his encounter with the Master renounces even his pen name. The names of the writers dancing at the Griboedov House restaurant, such as Bogokhulsky (the one who blasphemes), indicate that the narrator views this whole milieu as a hell of vulgarity, banality, and profanation of art. At midnight the famous Griboedov jazz band strikes up a fox trot; the jumping and tramping of all those Bogokhulskys and their dames presents such a diabolic picture that the narrator, deafened by the din, looks at them with fear and dismay.

The metaphor of hell appears on all levels of the novel through the juxtaposition of various segments of existence through time and space, revealing the presence of evil everywhere. The grotesque dancing at the Griboedov restaurant anticipates Voland's midnight ball, a real hell, where an unbearably loud jazz band strikes up a fox trot and Voland's "guests" dance: elegant gentlemen and naked ladies, criminals, murderers, sinners, whose decayed corpses have regained, for a few hours, by a diabolic magic, their former human shapes. A farcical "domestic hell" is suggested in the fantastic nightmare of Nikanor Bosoi: an investigator has released from prison a certain Sergei Dunchill just after his wife has seen his beautiful mistress to whom he had given valuable gifts, and sent him home to "the hell which your wife is preparing for you" (582). Another hell is evoked in a dream of Margarita, who sees the Master in prison-camp surroundings, so miserable and gloomy that one might easily be tempted to hang oneself, a "hell for a living person" (634). Finally, another kind of hell is also present in the novel—the moral hell of remorse and remembrance of past sin.

Voland and His Minions

The twofold nature of man, created good but everywhere overwhelmed by evil, is the source of numerous ambiguities in his existence. Ambiguities pervade the fantastic level of Bulgakov's novel. Devils representing various vices have frequently appeared in world literature. By introducing devils into his novel, Bulgakov gave reality a new dimension: he inserts fantasy, carnivalesque grotesquery, and phantasmagoria into the narrative texture and thus into everyday life. Indeed, very early on the work was called "a fantastic novel," and in one of its early drafts the prospective main hero, Fessia, studied medieval demonology.[4] Bulgakov himself read widely in demonology, sorcery, and magic.

From the many possible names of Satan, Bulgakov selected Voland, borrowed from Goethe's *Faust*.[5] Bulgakov created his own incarnation of the "prince of darkness," as he was called in the drafts of the novel. Voland's figure can be traced back to biblical texts, for example, to the Prophet Zechariah's apocalyptic vision in which Satan standing before the angel of the Lord figures as "the Adversary," is placed at the right hand of Joshua the high priest "to resist him," and is rebuked by the Lord (Zach. 3:1–4). Bulgakov's Voland is addressed by his retinue as "messire," which goes back to "messer Satanas," the usual term for the devil.

The Faustian connection is not limited to the names of Voland and Margarita; Goethe's immortal work pervades Bulgakov's novel more by its spirit than in concrete affinities, which have been studied in numerous articles.[6] The eternal basic motive of man's existence—temptation and resistance to evil—found a new interpretation in Bulgakov, whose Voland plays a different role than Mephistopheles. Ironically, Bulgakov gave his hero several theatrical accessories usually used in Gounod's opera *Faust,* such as a beret with a rooster feather, but they do not make Voland a comic figure or a "sympathetic" Satan. Voland's diabolic magic power, manifested in his eyes, is described several times. Voland's green eye provides him with knowledge of man's nature and his fate (also symbolized by the diamond triangle on his cigarette case and his watch). Voland's left eye, empty and black, symbolizes the eternal darkness of cosmic bottomlessness.

Voland is a biblical figure, not a Mephistophelian one. The novel contains hidden references to the Bible. The apparently strange fact of the communication between two "departments," as Voland puts it, and the ambiguous conversation between Matthew Levi and Voland, may be explained by reference to the Old Testament. Matthew Levi is sent to Voland by Yeshua to give him power over the Master's final fate, much in the tradition of the Book of Job, where the Lord converses with Satan and gives him power over his servant Job (Job 1:8–14). Also, in the Acts of Pontius Pilate (The Gospel of Nicodemus), known to Bulgakov, the soul of Christ descends to hell, where Satan, "the prince and captain of death," says that it was he, Satan, who stirred up the Jews against him (15:1, 8–10).

Now the devils are in Moscow, serving as a kind of catalyst to reveal man's evil intentions. The most important of them is the red-haired Azazello, Voland's closest helper. He appears as Margarita's "friend," with whom she will strike a diabolic bargain and who will poison her and the Master. The name Azazello—derived from the Hebrew word meaning "away," later understood as the demon of the wilderness and death—goes back to the Book of Leviticus. The jovial black cat Behemoth takes his name from the Book of Job, where the Lord says to Job: "Behold now behemoth, which I made with thee; he eateth grass as an ox . . ." (Job 40:15–24). In later mythology Behemoth was understood as a beast who could appear in the form of an ox, bull, or elephant, and represented the demon of gluttony. (At the foreign currency store Bulgakov's Behemoth swallows whole tangerines, chocolate bars with their gold wrappers, and herrings with heads [765]).

Koroviev-Fagot, another jester-devil, may be a variation on the bull symbolism, for Koroviev derives from the word for "cow" in Russian. He is associated with counterfeit money, which he plucks out of the air on several occasions. He may also be an ironic reference to Mephistopheles' singing of the hymn to the "Golden calf" in Gounod's *Faust*.

Only one devil—Abaddon (Greek Apollyon, Rev. 9:10), the angel of the bottomless pit and sovereign of locusts—preserves his apocalyptic image of sudden death. Not a member of Voland's retinue, he appears only twice: once before Satan's ball in Voland's room, to show Margarita the inevitability of death (675); and again at the end of the ball to execute Baron Maigel, a spy and denunciator (690).

The black devil-dog, derived from the medieval folk-legend of the magician Johannes Faust, who attained his fame as the black poodle that followed Heinrich Faust in Goethe's tragedy and was transformed into Mephistopheles, appears only as a poodle's head on Voland's cane (426), and as an adornment, in a frame on a heavy chain which Koroviev hangs on Margarita's neck (677). This adornment, which causes her pain, is a sign of her metamorphosis into the Queen of Satan's ball—a curious transformation of the traditional Grand Sabbath. At this ball, Bulgakov replaced repulsive details of traditional devils' and witches' Sabbath by a faerie with flowers, a Strauss waltz, and tropical butterflies and birds floating over the dancing couples. However, the essence of the diabolic assembly is the same—including the swamp smell and the drunken debauchery. Voland's "guests" are not a nightmarish product of Bosch's surrealistic imagination, but historical people, such as Caligula, Messalina, and many criminals subject to satanic evil in their earthly life. The ball presents a horrible picture of human corruption and immorality.

Although Bulgakov's devils, according to tradition, materialize from nowhere, change their shapes, cast no shadows, disappear suddenly, or become invisible, for the most part they act quite prosaically amid a prosaic ambience. More than that, Bulgakov uses the devils in numerous humorous episodes. For example, at their first appearance in apartment no. 50, they amuse themselves by mocking Stepa Likhodeev, the incompetent director of the Variety Theater; Behemoth stages a hilarious comedy when he surprises the plain clothes policemen, who has come to arrest the black magician's gang, with his famous statement: "I am doing no mischief, I don't bother anyone, I am repairing the kerosene burner" (758), and plays a series of pranks.

At the same time, in several fantastic-realistic grotesque scenes there is a submerged symbolism of death. On Saturday night the traditional black horses of death take Margarita, the Master, and Voland's entire gang to the realm of their supernatural existence. The diabolic masquerade ends during that flight: the devils lose their grotesque disguises and change their behavior. By the scarlet light of the full moon they recover their true forms. Margarita is especially surprised by her "dear" "protector" Azazello's transformation into a murderer with cold and empty black holes instead of eyes, the repulsive demon of the waterless desert and painful death.

Voland alone keeps his shape as a majestic dark ruler, whose black horse and black cape look now like a huge moon-pierced hulk of cosmic darkness. After a brief decisive talk with the Master and Margarita on the top of a rocky mountain, where Pilate was condemned to immortality, Voland rushes into a bottomless black abyss, taking with him his retinue and the unsolved mystery of his essence and destructive power.

The Drama of the Master

Though the image of the Master, the nameless writer, is rather passive, together with Margarita he occupies the central place in the novel. He enters the stage for the first time at the end of chapter 11, when he makes a night visit to his neighbor Ivan. He appears in four more chapters: in Margarita's dream (chapter 19); in chapter 24 he is summoned to Voland's bedroom after the satanic ball; in chapter 30 he is poisoned; and in chapter 31 he finds his "eternal refuge." Finally, in the epilogue he appears as a shadow in Ivan's dream.

The Master enters Ivan's hospital ward encouraged by Ivan's friendly attitude, and the two immediately reach a mutual understanding. When Ivan asks why his visitor does not escape since he has the keys to the balcony grills, the visitor replies that he has nowhere to go, which is the ultimate stage of man's loneliness and despair. He also has given up his name, like everything else in life.

When he learns that Ivan was sent to the clinic "because of Pontius Pilate," the visitor admits he is in the clinic because he has written a novel about Pilate but refuses to be called a writer. He declares: "I am a Master," puts on a black cap with the yellow embroidered letter "M," and tells Ivan his rather unusual story. A historian by education, he speaks five languages and used to work in one of the Moscow museums. His sudden winning of 100,000 rubles made it possible for him to rent a small apartment and devote himself completely to his novel. For him this time was "a golden age": by spring the novel was almost ready.

Then the Master met a wonderful woman: "Love caught us like a murderer jumping out of a dark alley," as he puts it (556). They knew that they were predestined for one another for eternity, though she was married. She came every day to see the Master and soon became his "secret friend." For several months the little apartment became their paradise on earth; it was she who called him "Master." All this is clearly based on the relationship between Bulgakov and Elena Shilovskaya, who became his "secret friend" in 1929, when he was thirty-eight, the age of his Master.

In August the Master finished his novel and wanted to publish it, but his contact with the literary world was a disaster. His editor read the novel and gave an evasive answer. Soon the critics Latunsky and Ahriman and a certain writer Mstislav Lavrovich viciously accused him of propagating religiosity and "Pilatism." The Master's story summarizes Bulgakov's own painful experience: Orlinsky's famous article "Against Bulgakovism" and the vicious slander campaign headed by Averbach (Ahriman), Blium, Litovsky, and others, after the performance of *The Days of the Turbins* and the preparation of *Flight*. Vsevolod Vishnevsky is the prototype of Mstislav Lavrovich. The dramatic scene in which the Master burns his novel replicates Bulgakov's own burning of his novel about the devil in March 1930. However, the Master's story also has larger implications and even foreshadows the fate of Boris Pasternak and his *Doctor Zhivago*.

The persecuted Master's fear of darkness and of a mystical octopus which threatens to strangle him with its tentacles is a foreboding of his arrest upon the denunciation of Aloisius Mogarych. One night he was taken away; what happened to him for the next three months the Master can only whisper in Ivan's ear. The truth of his whereabouts was suggested by Margarita's dream, in which she saw him in prison camp. When the Master returned, he found his little apartment occupied, and realized he had nowhere to go. His only refuge was a psychiatric clinic, another form of nonfreedom.

"I am incurable," the Master responds to Ivan's suggestion that he might recover. Once again the Master's story parallels Bulgakov's: through his hero Bulgakov confirmed his recognition that his disease was terminal. The motif of bidding farewell to life accompanies the Master. After his arrest, the Master did not write Margarita for fear of exposing her to the hardships of his maimed existence. And now he has found the moral strength to renounce the joy of meeting Margarita again. He had told this to Margarita during their last encounter, in trying to dissuade her from leaving her husband and coming to him: "I don't want you to perish here with me" (564).[7]

During his last months of life, the Master talks only to Ivan. Before his final disappearance the Master's shade comes to bid farewell to the former poet, now called Ivanushka, like the Russian fairytale hero, and ask him to write the continuation of the Master's novel. "Farewell, my disciple!" are the Master's last words said to a living being. A few moments later, the nurse tells Ivan that his nameless neighbor from ward 118 has just died.

In Margarita, Bulgakov created an attractive image of a loyal and courageous woman in the best Russian literary tradition. Her name evokes several literary associations, and she also has a prototype: the resemblances between Margarita and Bulgakov's wife Elena Sergeevna go far beyond the description of her beauty and her comfortable life in the luxurious home of her first husband. Like Margarita, Elena believed in Bulgakov's creative talent, encouraged him to re-create his destroyed novel, and years later fulfilled Voland's "prophecy" that "manuscripts do not burn" by ensuring posthumous fame for Bulgakov's last work.

Margarita is not only the embodiment of an ideal love. She is also able to defend her love and to sacrifice herself for her beloved. After she leaves him on the fatal night of his arrest, Margarita reproaches herself violently for leaving her beloved at such a moment (633). Her feeling of guilt and desperate desire to restore everything as it was before prompt her further actions. Moved to indignation by the injustice done to the Master, Margarita appeals to demonic power, exclaiming that she would "pawn my soul to the devil to find out whether he is still alive or not!" (639). Azazello appears in response to her cry, and then she, like Faust, strikes a bargain with the devil, since only supernatural evil could help her to overcome real evil and to find out her beloved's fate.

Her sudden transformation into an invisible witch with the help of Azazello's magic ointment makes it possible for her to take revenge on the critic Latunsky, who ruined the Master's life. But she does not use her diabolic power for evil purposes. Margarita always preserves her positive human qualities—love, compassion, and longing for mercy.

Why, one may ask, did these two suffering persons not earn the light so that they could be taken into the realm of Yeshua and Matthew Levi? The persecution that the Master endured made him face the metaphysical evil inherent in everyday life without the visible presence of satanic agents. Unable to fight organized slander, the Master renounces his own personality as he has renounced life. When he appears before Voland, the presence of Satan overwhelms him with anguish and fear. Even the sight of Margarita does not help him overcome this fear: his exclamation, "Even by moonlight at night there is no rest for me, why did they trouble me? Oh gods, gods . . ." (703), parallels the complaint of Pilate, his hero.[8]

The Master, who punishes his Pilate because "cowardice was the most terrible sin of all" (735), recognizes shortly before his death that he is also guilty of pusillanimity. More than that, the Master has lost faith in men as well as in life. He is overcome by despair, the gravest of the seven deadly sins. When Behemoth restores his novel from the ashes, the Master repudiates it for the second time: "I hate this novel," he says to Voland. "I have suffered too much because of it" (708). And since he hates his novel, the Master also repudiates his own heroes, Pilate and Yeshua. That is why Margarita asks Voland not only to return her and the Master back to their beloved apartment, but to make "everything as it was" (704) in the period before the Master repudiated his own life and work.

Ambiguity pervades the novel to the very end—to the mysterious disappearance of the bodies of the Master and Margarita after their death. When the Master dies on Saturday at sunset, Margarita collapses at the same time at her home (785–86). But they also die, poisoned by Azazello, after their happy reunion in the Master's apartment. It could be, as the text suggests, that everything that happens to Margarita after she rereads the half-burned pages of the Master's manuscript—her transformation into a witch, her flight, her presence at Voland's satanic ball, and the miraculous evocation of the Master—is only a dream. After they return to the Master's study, "where all was as it had been before the terrible autumn night of the last year" (713–14), Margarita is suddenly seized by panic that "all this is nothing more than sorcery."

But even if it is only a dream, by the intensity of her love Margarita reaches the supernatural realm and thus communicates with the Master. And he himself feels it through his dream: while in Voland's room, he remarks that everything he sees there seems a hallucination (702). The Master and Margarita both exist in two dimensions: their physical existence is tied to realities, his to the clinic, hers to the "gothic" villa. But their souls move in an unlimited space.

At the end the Master is reunited forever with his beloved Margarita, and he seems to have attained the things he most values: a calm conscience and a peaceful, quiet refuge. But he has paid for it by a complete obliteration of his past, of his novel and his heroes:

as soon as the Master and Margarita cross the stream, they plunge into soundlessness and impending oblivion. The Master and Margaita have escaped the world of evil, but, unable to reach the realm of light, like Dante's pre-Christian spirits, they will remain in a kind of limbo which, in some aspects, is closer to the Dantean Garden of Eden, where Lethe removes the memory of past sin along with the memory of past suffering.[9]

Yeshua and Pilate

The Master's story of Pilate and Yeshua forms the basic part of Bulgakov's novel and carries the author's main ethical message. Bulgakov pursues two basic aims in the "ancient" chapters of the novel: first—to refute Mikhail Berlioz's "main point" that Jesus had never existed and that "all the stories about him were invention, simple myth" (425); and second, to show that the spirit of Jesus, vividly evoked in the transfigured image of the vagrant philosopher Yeshua, as well as Pilate's sin, persist through the centuries.

Through the Master's novel, Bulgakov set in modern terms problems that were most acutely framed almost two thousand years earlier: the struggle of Good and Evil, the cruelty of executing an innocent, remorse over a crime, the meanness of betrayal, and the attempt to expiate sin by an act of mercy.

As a religious man and a Christian, Bulgakov did not permit himself to rewrite or to paraphrase the Gospels. He was interested in the historical Jesus and the historical Pilate. Therefore, using his artistic imagination he depicted the events as they could have happened in the historical Yershalaim, at the time of the cruel Claudius Nero Tiberius, Roman emperor from 14 to 37 A.D.

It should be noted that Bulgakov did not touch the kerygma of Christ: he stopped at the burial of the Crucified. His was a secular work; the connection of the historical Jesus and the Christ in the kerygma, the resurrected Lord and Savior, belongs to theology.[10] Thus Bulgakov did not even refer to the Gospels, although he dealt with the same events described there.

The search for the historical Jesus has gone on for years, conducted by both believers and nonbelievers. Bulgakov was well acquainted with ancient historical writings such as Josephus Flavius's *The Jewish War*, Tertullian's *Apology*, Suetonius Tranquillus's *Twelve Caesars*, and Cornelius Tacitus's *Annals* and *History*. Numerous works on the life of Jesus were written in the centuries following.[11] Many of them—especially those by David Friedrich Strauss and by Ernest Renan—were popular in Russia and provided a number of details which Bulgakov undoubtedly knew. He was also well versed in the apocryphal Gospel of Nicodemus, which contains historical facts and data.[12]

In four artistically superb chapters Bulgakov affirmed the historical existence of a young philosopher named Yeshua Hah Notsri (Yeshua from Nazareth). In his "ancient" chapters (2—"Pontius Pilate"; 6—"The Execution"; 25—"How the Procurator tried to Save Judas of Karioth"; and 26—"The Burial") Bulgakov demythologized the factual events and stressed their historical reality.

Roman military rule over the Jewish population created constant tension which occasionally surfaced in local rebellions. Pilate has to obey the imperial orders not to violate the religious customs of the Jews. Since he has already been accused by the Jewish priests of disregarding these orders, he is especially annoyed by a case like that of Yeshua, who was arrested and condemned by the Jewish priests and delivered to him for a final verdict.

At the interrogation Pilate appears in a white cloak with a blood-red lining and suffers from acute pains in the left side of his head, a sign of the presence of a diabolic spirit: the Master and Margarita also feel an ache in the left temple shortly before Azazello comes to poison them. Events are presented as Pilate saw them at the interrogation: all that had happened to Yeshua before his final encounter with Pilate, such as the Sanhedrin trial and death sentence, is only mentioned.

Three different world views confront one another here: the inflexible Jewish Law, any deviation from which is considered a threat to all of Israel; Roman pragmatic rationalism, when military and state power justified merciless acts; and the ethics of the vagrant philosopher Yeshua, who preaches the inherent goodness of man and the establishment of a kingdom of truth and justice.

Pilate knows the Sanhedrin will force him to confirm its death sentence, but his sense of justice protests against executing a man who has committed no crime. Listening to the accused, Pilate feels the spell of his extraordinary personality. But as soon as he is informed of Yeshua's alleged "seditious" speeches, Pilate realizes that he has no choice.

Judas from Karioth has already denounced Yeshua as a political anti-Roman subversive for declaring that the time would come when "man will pass into kingdom of truth and justice" where no power will be needed (447). The spiritual meaning of Yeshua's words has been twisted into a statement directed against Roman political power and Jewish religious law, and Yeshua has been arrested by the Sanhedrin's agents. All Pilate's efforts to suggest to Yeshua that he must refute this denunciation only cause Yeshua to attack power as a form of violence imposed upon people. That is enough to constitute the worst possible crime at the time of Tiberius: offending the Augustinian divinity of the Roman emperor. Pilate suddenly feels a vague desire to escape his responsibilities through suicide, an honorable death at the time of Tiberius' tyrannical rule.[13] Pilate knows now that both he and the accused are in danger: if he releases Yeshua, the high priest Caiphas will denounce him to Tiberius. Thus, reasons of state as well as his own cowardice cause the mighty Roman governor to become an instrument of evil in the hands of Yershalaim's rulers. The experienced politicians Annas and Caiphas shift the entire responsibility to Pilate for pronouncing the final word of condemnation.

Chapter 16 describes the crucifixion in minute historical detail. The presence of Matthew Levi at the Bald Mountain, instead of the biblical figure of Joseph of Arimathea, intensifies the drama. Prevented from joining Yeshua the evening before by a sudden illness, Matthew seeks to expiate his involuntary failure by stabbing Yeshua to end his suffering and then killing himself. Unable to do it, he stays near the cross until the very end; then, covered by darkness and pouring rain, it is he, the true disciple, who takes the body of his Master from the cross to give him the last rites.

At the moment of the crucifixion, Pilate is in his residence in the city. Irritated, he smashes a jug of wine, and a blood-red puddle spreads at his feet, into which the storm throws two white roses. The puddle will never vanish, and the symbolic white roses will constantly remind Pilate of his crime. Here begins Pilate's mystery play presented in the two last chapters of the Master's novel, an astonishing artistic blend of historically verisimilar events and a mystical symbolic thought.

Pilate first attempts to shorten Yeshua's suffering on the cross, but his order reaches the Bald Mountain too late. Then, Pilate tries to quell his conscience by ordering secret agents to kill Judas the informer.

Pilate's conversation with a mysterious man in a hood—Aphranius, head of his secret service—is a brilliant piece of psychological interplay in which almost every sentence has a real meaning which is the opposite of its apparent meaning, and this is well understood by both interlocutors. Besides, both, to cover themselves, intersperse their statements with assurances of their loyalty to the great Caesar.

The episode with Judas of Karioth is a legend created by Bulgakov but apparently suggested by a passage in the Acts of the Apostles (1:16–18), according to which Judas died by accident, with no remorse, "falling headlong, he burst asunder in the midst" of the field of blood purchased with the reward of his denunciation. In the novel, Judas is killed by Aphranius's agents in the garden of Gethsemane, where he had betrayed Yeshua (732–33).

Nevertheless the death of Judas, into whom "Satan entered" (John 13:27),[14] does not free Pilate from the nagging thought that "this morning he had irretrievably lost something" (725). His desire to recapture what he has lost is so intense that it becomes part of a dream in which he talks to the vagrant philosopher alive, who confirms that there has been no execution, nor could there have been.

All this remains only a beautiful dream. Still, Pilate's repentance opens for him the way to moral regeneration: the cruel, skeptical Roman procurator is granted the capacity to distinguish good from evil; Christian forgiveness and belief in the presence of goodness in man's heart become accessible to him.

In his novel Bulgakov vividly evoked the historical environment and circumstances of those days and also suggested the possible behavior of the personages involved in the drama. He brought the past to life to show how crucial events of the past, which influenced the entire development of Western civilization, continue to have relevance for our own day.

Thus our analysis shows that the structure of this complex novel, the genre of which can hardly be defined in traditional terms, has been almost mathematically calculated and perfectly elaborated. All four main plot lines merge at the end to establish the unity of all aspects of man's existence and the author's intent. The shifts in time and space help to establish the far-reaching affinities between the events that took place in ancient Jerusalem and the passing of Easter in the Moscow of the 1930s. Nothing can prevent the human mind from escaping the banality of everyday life into the realm of the supernatural. Man's search for truth and justice never ceases, although it sometimes takes unusual forms. The Master and Margarita, and later Ivan, escape their suffering through contact with the supernatural—at first demonic, then metaphysical—and reach the sphere of spiritual knowledge. The Gospel texts are sacred, and Bulgakov did not attempt to paraphrase them. He wrote a variation on the well-known subject and created his own apocrypha. By relating it to contemporary life, he reminded his readers of the everlasting spiritual value of the dramatic events that took place in ancient Jerusalem.

Chapter Eight
Later Plays and Stage Adaptations

Alexander Pushkin or *Last Days*

The theme of a great writer struggling against implacable fate, slander, and the banning of his works reemerges in the play *Alexander Pushkin* (1934–35). After Bulgakov's death, the play was re-titled *Poslednie dni (Last Days)* for performance at the Moscow Art Theater in 1943.

Bulgakov conceived the idea of a play about Pushkin's last days during painfully sporadic rehearsals of his play on Molière at the Art Theater, and he eventually gave *Pushkin* to the Vakhtangov Theater. The theater historian Vitaly Vilenkin reports that the Art Theater hoped to produce *Pushkin* for the centennial of Pushkin's death.[1] Unfortunately, in Bulgakov's lifetime *Pushkin* was never staged.

Bulgakov decided to write a play about Pushkin without Pushkin, which may seem surprising but is fully justified. Pushkin is familiar to Russians from their earliest school years. To Bulgakov, a Pushkin on stage would be a profanation of the now almost legendary image of Russia's greatest poet. His physical presence on stage is hinted at three times and described in the stage directions: in act 1 he slips into his study like a shadow; in act 2, at the ball, he stands hardly visible behind a column; and finally in act 4 he is taken home for his last hours.

Each of the four acts in Bulgakov's play consists of several scenes separated by moments of darkness enveloping the stage. In act 1 the action occurs at the end of January and in early February of 1837 in Alexander Pushkin's drawing room in St. Petersburg and in the dining room of the famous bibliophile Sergei Saltykov. In Pushkin's apartment, Alexandra Goncharova, sister of his wife Nathalie, pays off an insistent creditor with her own jewelry. Alexandra receives an anonymous letter which insults Pushkin, but Nathalie pays no attention to it; she has been accompanied home by her *beau-frère* d'Anthès. Frightened at the idea of her husband's seeing him, she promises d'Anthès a rendezvous. At Saltykov's home, the popular playwright Nestor Kukolnik introduces the romantic poet Vladimir Benediktov. Kukolnik and Prince Peter Dolgorukov denigrate Pushkin and proclaim Benediktov Russia's foremost poet.

Act 2 opens at a ball in the winter garden of Count Vorontsov's palace. The Emperor Nikolai I has a brief conversation with Nathalie Pushkina as a Prince Dolgorukov spies on them. Baron Heeckeren, the Dutch ambassador, and his adopted son George d'Anthès approach Nathalie and compel her to promise d'Anthès a rendezvous. Dolgorukov and a secret agent, Bogomazov, comment on the conversation they have just overheard and again criticize Pushkin until Countess Vorontsova, a fervent admirer of Pushkin's poetry, asks Dolgorukov to leave her house. At His Majesty's Chancellery, the chief of the gendarme section, General Leonty Dubelt, receives information on Pushkin from secret agents Bitkov and Bogomazov. Nikolai I appears with Count Benckendorf, chief of the Third Section of the Imperial Chancellery. They discuss a prospective duel between Pushkin and d'Anthès, and a satirical poem of Pushkin. Benckendorf orders Dubelt to arrest both of the prospective duelists, adding that the place of the duel may be changed.[2]

In act 3 the action reaches its climax in three crucial scenes. Baron Heeckeren receives an insulting letter from Pushkin and reads some passages to his friend Count Stroganov. Baron Heeckeren, as a diplomat, cannot challenge Pushkin to a duel, and Count Stroganov suggests that Baron d'Anthès challenge Pushkin, because a duel is the only possible answer to the letter. The next scene takes place on a bridge where Baron Heeckeren is awaiting the outcome of the duel when d'Anthès appears, slightly wounded. In the third scene, in Pushkin's apartment, everybody awaits the poet, who has told his old servant Nikita that he "went for a ride with Danzas." This news puts his friend, the poet Vasily Zhukovsky, on the alert. Danzas enters as the servants carry in the mortally wounded poet. Act 4 shows the aftermath of Pushkin's death. Dubelt and the gendarmes are present as Pushkin's coffin is borne out in front of huge crowds. The final scene takes place at night, at a remote post-station. Pushkin's coffin is taken to the Sviatogorsky monastery near his small estate in the village of Mihailovskoe. Only his friend

Alexander Turgenev and his loyal servant Nikita are allowed to escort Pushkin's coffin on the poet's final journey.

Bulgakov's play is not a strictly documentary biographical study, but a drama created on the basis of historical facts. As he did for Molière, Bulgakov studied documents, letters, and memoirs of Pushkin's contemporaries. Bulgakov's correspondence with the writer Vikenty Veresaev, author of a book on Pushkin's life, shows how carefully Bulgakov adapted historical facts to fit theatrical requirements.[3]

Many scenes and episodes are based on real events in the life of St. Petersburg high society while others are fictional but help re-create the ambience of the poet's last days. Thus, the ball at the palace of Count Ivan Vorontsov-Dashkov did in fact take place on 23 January 1837, and his wife did admire Pushkin's poetry. Furthermore, according to Konstantin Danzas's eyewitness report the gendarmes were sent to the wrong place; otherwise their timely arrival would have prevented the duel. Danzas also named Prince Peter Dolgorukov as the author of insulting anonymous letters sent to Pushkin and his friends.[4] Among the cast of characters, only the two police informers Bitkov and Bogomazov are fictitious.

Two major motifs underlie the entire action of Bulgakov's play: the imminence of the duel and Pushkin's growing fame as Russia's foremost poet. The letters and diaries of Pushkin's contemporaries show that only a few people realized the dramatic tension of the situation. Among them was Pushkin's friend Prince Peter Viazemsky, who wrote shortly after the duel that "a fatal predestination drove Pushkin toward ruin."[5]

In the play, Pushkin's servant Nikita is the first to express his concern when he asks Alexandra to persuade Pushkin to leave the capital for the country: "There's not going to be anything good in St. Petersburg" (293). General Dubelt is sure that a duel is imminent after he reads the draft of Pushkin's letter to Baron Heeckeren which Bogomazov has brought him (327). The final judgment is pronounced by the blind Count Stroganov, uncle of Nathalie Pushkina. Informing the count about Pushkin's letter, Baron Heeckeren still insists that George d'Anthès "had not given any cause" for Pushkin's accusations. Count Stroganov expresses the opinion of high society in saying that now "it no longer makes any difference whether Baron d'Anthès gave him reasons or not"; only a duel is possible (355).

Pushkin's fame and the grief of the people come to the surface at the news of his death, when huge crowds gather in front of his home to pay their last respects. A student climbs a street lantern to read out loud Mikhail Lermontov's famous poem on Pushkin's death; an army officer shouts to the crowd that Pushkin was murdered. Vasily Zhukovsky, himself an outstanding poet, clearly understands Pushkin's importance, as does the young Countess Vorontsova. Even the uneducated informer Bitkov is fascinated by the poem "The storm covers the sky with darkness."

Throughout the play a snowstorm serves as background for the action. In act 1, a snowstorm is heard in Pushkin's apartment as an evil omen. At the end, Pushkin's verses about the howling wind and sky covered with darkness, recited by Bitkov to the stationmaster's wife, symbolize the poet's immortality. He may be buried in a distant cemetery, but his voice will resound through the centuries.

Don Quixote

Bulgakov's stage adaptation of Cervantes's novel *Don Quixote* deals with a similar subject—the plight and death of an idealist slandered by his contemporaries. Bulgakov did the main work on it in the summer of 1938, immediately after finishing *The Master and Margarita*. In this play Bulgakov again expressed his concern with man's search for truth and justice, and so, it is appropriate to examine it as a variation on the themes of *Molière, Alexander Pushkin,* and *The Master and Margarita.*

Don Quixote premiered at the Bolshoi Drama Theater in Leningrad on 13 March 1941, a year after Bulgakov's death, and a few weeks later at the Vakhtangov Theater in Moscow. Critics generally have taken a positive view of Bulgakov's adaptation.[6]

Bulgakov defined his approach in the subtitle "A Play According to Cervantes." Thus it is not an exact adaptation of some parts of the novel, but the playwright's own concept of Cervantes' heroes, Don Quixote and Sancho Panza, in the most popular episodes of the novel infused into four acts (nine scenes). The play describes Don Quixote departing from his home with Sancho at his side; his fight with the windmills; his attack on the monks; the encounter with the Yanguesian carriers who badly beat the knight and his squire; the adventure in the inn with the famous balm; the adventures at the duke's castle as well as Sancho governing "his island."

Bulgakov also introduces some scenes with no counterpart in Cervantes' novel: for example, he extended the part of Don Quixote's niece Antonia, adding a romance with Samson Carrasco, and had Aldonza—"Dulcinea" appear on stage. Bulgakov highlights dialogues during which both the knight and his squire reveal their philosophy of life.

Bulgakov's Don Quixote is an idealist who views himself as a follower of a religious order, as suggested by Cervantes in the second part of his novel. Don Quixote wants to restore justice. In his conversation with the clergyman in the duke's castle, Don Quixote says that he has righted injustice, and that he intends to do good to all the world (434). Defeated by the bachelor Samson Carrasco, disguised as "the Knight of the White Moon," Don Quixote still remains faithful to his ideals of honor, pure love, and compassion for the injured and humiliated. But he is cured of his mad fancies and faces reality: "I am no longer Don Quixote de la Mancha, but Alonso Quixano, called the Good" (460). He is forced by the "cruel knight" to return to his village forever, and not just for a year, as in the novel. Now Don Quixote feels that along with his impossible dreams he has lost his freedom, which is, as he tells Sancho, "the most precious treasure that man was granted" (456). Bulgakov altered the conclusion: in the final scene his Don Quixote feels that his last day has come, and the sunset will be followed by engulfing darkness, in an image that recalls the closing scene in *The Master and Margarita*. Thus, in this stage adaptation Bulgakov succeeded "in making the play his own," as A. Colin Wright has aptly remarked.[7]

Batum

Bulgakov's last play, *Batum,* written in 1939, stands apart from his other works. It contains none of the leitmotivs typical of his earlier stories and plays, nor does it reach Bulgakov's usual artistic standard.

According to two Soviet specialists, Bulgakov intended to write a play, "A Pastor," as early as March 1936.[8] He abandoned it, but in 1939 returned to it at the insistence of his friends at the Moscow Art Theater. However, he did it reluctantly and expressed doubts about the feasibility in general of producing a play on Stalin's youth.

As his main sources Bulgakov used memoirs of Stalin's contemporaries and archival documents on underground communist activities and workers unrest in Batum in 1902–4. The plot revolves around the young revolutionary Joseph Dzhugashvili-Stalin and his role in worker uprisings in the Caucasus at that time. It consists of four acts and covers several years. A prologue scene in which Joseph Dzhugashvili is expelled from a theological seminary for his participation in an underground antigovernmental organization takes place in 1898. Three years later Stalin, now known as "comrade Soso," finds refuge from police surveillance in the house of Silvester, a Batum worker, as he organizes workers for revolutionary activities. In act 2, scenes 5 and 6 show a workers' meeting at the Rothschild factory, which has been half destroyed by arsonists, and the ensuing confrontation between the workers and the authorities. The military governor orders the arrest of several workers, whose liberation the other workers demand the next day as they clash with the police. A military unit summoned by the authorities kills or wounds several workers. Among the wounded is Silvester's son Porfiry. In act 3, Stalin is arrested at the apartment of the revolutionary worker Darispan. In the second scene of this act, one year later, the imprisoned criminals help Stalin to send letters out of the prison and to talk to Silvester's daughter Natasha. A prison guard strikes Natasha, which, at Stalin's signal, provokes a unanimous prisoner protest. At the governor's order Stalin is transferred to another prison. Act 4 presents Emperor Nicholas II in his office. The minister of justice reports that, by imperial law, Dzhugashvili should be exiled to eastern Siberia for three years for crimes against the state. In the closing scene two months later, Porfiry and Natasha, both back from prison at their father's house in Batum, are wondering why they have no news from the exiled Dzhugashvili when suddenly Stalin reappears, returned to resume his revolutionary activities among Caucasian workers.

Batum lacks originality. Such scenes as the search and Stalin's arrest or the workers' protest meetings derive from typical scenes described in many revolutionary works, such as Maxim Gorky's novel *The Mother* or Nikolay Ostrovsky's *How the Steel Was Tempered*. There is no character development. Stalin is the central character, the revolutionary leader, the "wise man," the "Pastor," but he is hardly heroic. Though the other characters coordinate their activities with his acts and words, he nevertheless greatly depends on them. Silvester, Porfiry, and Natasha protect "comrade Soso" and hide him in their house, as does Darispan. The young Stalin is motivated not only by his revolutionary beliefs and the urge to overthrow the Russian monarchy, but also by the desire to avenge his humiliations in his continuous struggle with the authorities and especially with a certain police chief.

However, even this play displays flashes of Bulgakov's comic and satirical brilliance; for example, in the scene with the governor who cannot grasp the seriousness of the situation in Batum. Instead of paying attention to the managers' and police reports of worker unrest at several oil refineries and factories, the governor carps about the style of the reports. He blames the chief of the Batum police for reporting that over 300 workers were dismissed at the factory without indicating the cause of their dismissals, "its sense and meaning."[9] Dramatic suspense is high in the play's last scene, when Porfiry worries about Stalin's fate. When there is a knock at the window, Porfiry is terribly anxious about who it might be, and Stalin is so fearful that he does not dare tell Porfiry his name. Obviously such an image could not have pleased the all-powerful dictator of the 1930s. Thus the whole idea of a play on Stalin's youth was doomed to failure.

Adaptations

Out of Bulgakov's several adaptations of works by Nikolai Gogol for stage and screen, only one—his dramatization of *Dead Souls*—reached a large audience. Premiered in November 1932, the play has remained in the repertory of the Moscow Art Theater ever since. In 1934–35 Bulgakov wrote several versions of a filmscript based on *Dead Souls,* and another based on the comedy *The Inspector General,* but these films were never produced.[10]

Bulgakov's attitude toward Gogol is a complex subject deserving of special study.[11] Here we will note only that when Bulgakov was first asked to adapt *Dead Souls* for the stage, he planned to make Gogol his "First" character, the narrator who would introduce Chichikov and other personages. As Gogol wrote *Dead Souls* in Rome, Bulgakov envisioned placing Gogol in that setting, but Stanislavsky rejected the scene with Gogol in Rome as well as several eccentric and grotesque scenes, insisting on a realistic reproduction of well-known episodes. Bulgakov eventually wrote five versions of the play before he satisfied the directors of the Art Theater. Bulgakov's original conception of the play using music and sound effects has been described by Vasily Sakhnovsky in his *Rabota rezhissera* (Work of a producer, 1937) and by Bulgakov himself in private letters.[12] The result of Bulgakov's work was a series of skillfully compiled realistic episodes from Gogol's famous novel.

Bulgakov's stage adaptation of *War and Peace*, written in 1931–32 for the Bolshoi Drama Theater in Leningrad, was never produced either there or at the Moscow Art Theater.[13]

At the end of 1936 Bulgakov accepted a position as consultant-librettist at the Bolshoi Theater of Opera and Ballet and wrote several opera libretti: *Minin and Pozharsky* (1936–38), *The Black Sea* (1937), *Peter I* (1937), and *Rachel* (1939). Three of these were written on historical subjects. Only "The Black Sea" dealt with a contemporary theme: it is in fact a variation on the subject of Bulgakov's play *Flight,* on the battle in the Crimea between the Red forces and General Wrangel's White Army. After Bulgakov's death the libretto *Rachel* was used by the composer Reinhold Glier for a one-act patriotic opera performed in 1943 over the radio and by the actors of the Stanislavsky Opera Theater at a concert hall in 1947. The opera *Minin and Pozharsky,* with music by the Leningrad composer Boris Asafiev, was never produced on stage, though some scenes were performed in late 1938 by the choir and orchestra of the Radio Committee in Leningrad. This libretto, along with the correspondence between Bulgakov and Asafiev, was published in Moscow in 1980. The letters from 1936 to 1938 show how much effort the two excellent artists put into this opera, and also reflect their disappointment when the opera was rejected by the State Committee for the Arts.[14] The fact that while engaged in this frustrating and exhausting work Bulgakov continued to write his major novel bears witness to his courage as well as his creative and moral strength.

Chapter Nine

Conclusion

Indeed, courage, moral strength, and creative stamina are the characteristic and most striking features of Mikhail Bulgakov's personality. A talented man gifted with an exuberant imagination and an acute sense of historical reality, Bulgakov added impressive pages to the treasury of Russian literature. In his works Bulgakov never ceased to protest against the injustice, cruelty, and violence he had witnessed during the Civil War. Like certain of his contemporaries, Bulgakov used humor and satire to overcome anxiety in difficult historical periods. He transformed many morbid, absurd episodes and phenomena of the revolutionary and postrevolutionary years into comic and sometimes grotesque stories. Bulgakov's satire exhibits a skillful blend of fantastic and realistic elements, a combination of comedy and tragedy with important ethical issues that were always his main concern.

Bulgakov never had the time or appropriate circumstances to develop his multifaceted talent freely. Pressure from the authorities and politically motivated attacks by hostile critics made Bulgakov's life scarcely bearable. As his biography shows, he had frequently scarcely signed a contract and begun working on a play or a prose piece when he was suddenly informed that his contract had been canceled with no reason given. Now it is easy for critics to say that the stage fate of some of Bulgakov's plays turned to be "unhappy." But even the best scholars and critics, such as Pavel Markov, omit mention of the real reasons for the rejection or cancellation of Bulgakov's plays. However, Bulgakov's correspondence reveals what a devastating effect such treatment had on his health and state of mind. As he wrote in his letters, he suffered from acute nervous exhaustion and frustration. Nevertheless, even when his eyesight was failing Bulgakov continued to write. He drew from his own experience the drama of censored playwrights and the tragic destiny of writers fighting for spiritual and artistic independence, themes that occupy such an important place in Bulgakov's creation.

Bulgakov's last novel, *The Master and Margarita,* surprised everyone by the depth of the ethical issues it posed, its artistic perfection, and its stylistic variety. But a survey of Bulgakov's life and an analysis of his works show that this novel synthesizes many ideas and features that had already been dealt with in his previous works. Now the majority of writers, critics, and readers second the opinion expressed by Michael Glenny as early as 1967 that this novel "may well come to be regarded as the glory of twentieth-century Russian literature."[15]

Notes and References

Chapter One

1. Konstantin Paustovskii, "Bulgakov i teatr" (Bulgakov and the theater), in *Naedine s osen'iu* (Alone with autumn) (Moscow: Sovetskii pisatel', 1967), 151. First published in *Mosty* (Bridges) (Munich), no. 11 (1965):378–88.

2. "Avtobiografiia" (Autobiography), in *Sovetskie pisateli: Avtobiografii* (Soviet writers: autobiographies) (Moscow, 1966), 3:85.

3. "Spravka" (Certificate), quoted from *Neizdannyi Bulgakov: teksty i materialy* (Unpublished Bulgakov: texts and materials), ed. Ellendea Proffer (Ann Arbor: Ardis, 1977), 13.

4. Interview with Tatiana Nikolaevna Lappá, quoted from *Neizdannyi Bulgakov* (Unpublished Bulgakov), 18. See also T. Kisel'gof, "Gody molodosti" (Years of youth), as recorded by M. Chudakova, *Literaturnaia gazeta* (Literary gazette), 13 May 1981.

5. Quoted from M. Chudakova, "K tvorcheskoi biografii M. Bulgakova" (Toward a creative biography of M. Bulgakov), *Voprosy literatury* (Problems of literature), no. 7 (1973):234.

6. "Pis'ma k rodnym" (Letters to relatives), published by Elena Zemskaia in *Izvestiia Akademii nauk: Seriia literatury i iazyka* (News of the Academy of Sciences: literature and language series) 35, no. 5 (1976):454.

7. "Avtobiografiia" (Autobiography), 3:85.

8. "Pis'ma k rodnym" (Letters to relatives), 450.

9. "Avtobiografiia" (Autobiography), 3:85–86.

10. Nikolai Gorchakov, *Rezhisserskie uroki K. S. Stanislavskogo (Stanislavsky Directs)* (Moscow: Iskusstvo, 1951), 317–18.

11. A. Orlinskii, "Grazhdanskaia voina na stsene MKhAT" (The civil war on the Art Theater stage), *Pravda* (Truth), 8 October 1926; see also his "Protiv bulgakovshchiny" (Against Bulgakovism), *Novyi zritel'* (New spectator), no. 41 (1926):3.

12. A. V. Lunacharskii, "Pervye novinki sezona" (First new plays of the season), *Izvestiia* (News), 8 October 1926. See also O. Litovskii, " 'Dni Turbinykh' v Moskovskom Khudozhestvennom teatre" (*Days of the Turbins* at the Moscow Art Theater) (1926), quoted from Litovskii, *Glazami sovremennika* (Through the eyes of a contemporary) (Moscow: Sovetskii pisatel', 1963), 227; and M. Levidov, "Dosadnyi pustiak" (An irritating piece of trivia), *Vecherniaia Moskva* (Evening Moscow), 8 October 1926.

13. Viktor Petelin, "M. A. Bulgakov i 'Dni Turbinykh' " (Bulgakov and *Days of the Turbins*), *Ogonek* (Flame), no. 11 (March 1969):26. This is the longest and most accurate report of the public discussion of Bulgakov's play. The report of this discussion published in the 10 February 1927 issue of *Pravda* (Truth) was tendentious: while the speeches of Lunacharsky and Orlinsky were presented favorably, Bulgakov's speech was dismissed as "an attempt to rehabilitate his play."

14. Pavel Markov, "Bulgakov," introduction to Bulgakov, *P'esy* (Plays) (Moscow, 1962), 10.

15. Iakov Elsberg, "Bulgakov i MKhAT" (Bulgakov and the Moscow Art Theater), *Na literaturnom postu* (On literary guard), no. 2 (3 November 1927):44–49.

16. See the "Resolution of the Main Repertory Committee for 9 May 1928," as published by Ellendea Proffer in *Russian Literature Triquarterly*, no. 7 (1973):461–62.

17. "Obsuzhdenie p'esy M. A. Bulgakova 'Beg' " (Minutes of the discussion of M. A. Bulgakov's play *Flight* [at the Moscow Art Theater, 9 October 1928]) as published in *Russian Literature Triquarterly*, no. 7 (1973):464.

18. I. Turkeltaub, " 'Bagrovyi ostrov' v Moskovskom kamernom teatre" (*The Crimson Island* at the Moscow Kamernyi Theater), *Zhizn' iskusstva* (Life of art), no. 52 (1928):10.

19. Stalin's letter in response to Bill-Belotserkovskii was first published in his *Sochineniia* (Works) (Moscow: Politicheskaia literatura, 1949), 11:326–29.

20. Bulgakov's letters to Gorky and A. Enukidze have been published by Lesley Milne, "K biografii M. A. Bulgakova" (Toward a biography of Bulgakov), *Novyi zhurnal* (New review), no. 111 (1973):153–54.

21. The letter to A. P. Gdeshinskii of October 1929 is quoted from Marietta Chudakova, "Arkhiv M. A. Bulgakova" (The Bulgakov archive), *Zapiski Otdela rukopisei Vsesoiuznoi biblioteki im. Lenina,* (Transactions of the manuscript division of the All-Union Lenin Library, no. 37) (Moscow, 1976), 85.

22. Liubov' Belozerskaia-Bulgakova, *O, med vospominanii* (Oh, sweet reminiscences) (Ann Arbor; 1979), 99–100. Excerpts from this letter were published by S. Liandres, "Russkii pisatel' ne mozhet zhit' bez Rodiny" (A Russian writer cannot live in exile), *Voprosy literatury* (Problems of literature), no. 9 (1966):138–39; and the complete text in the newspaper *Posev* (Sowing), 29 September 1967, 3–4, and in the magazine *Grani* (Facets), no. 66 (1967):155–61 (both periodicals are published in Frankfurt am Main). The letter has been translated into English by L. M. Tikos, "A Russian Writer Speaks to Stalin," *Dissent*, May–June 1969, 271–74.

23. "Pis'ma M. A. Bulgakova P. S. Popovu" (M. A. Bulgakov's letters to P. S. Popov), *Teatr* (Theater), no. 5 (May 1981):92–93.

24. Zh. Molier, *Sobranie sochinenii* (Collected works), ed. A. A. Smirnov and S. S. Mokulskii, vol. 3 (Leningrad: Academia, 1939).

25. Osaf Litovskii, "Dva spektaklia" (Two performances), *Sovetskoe iskusstvo* (Soviet art), 11 February 1936.

26. Boris Alpers, "Reaktsionnye domysly M. Bulgakova" (Bulgakov's reactionary fantasies), *Literaturnaia gazeta* (Literary gazette), 10 March 1936.

27. "Kurs istorii SSSR" (A history of the U.S.S.R. [notes from the drafts]), published by A. Colin Wright in *Novyi zhurnal* (New review), no. 143 (1981):54–88.

28. Quoted from Chudakova, "Arkhiv M. A. Bulgakova" (The Bulgakov archive), 132.

29. V. Vilenkin, "O Mikhaile Afanas'eviche Bulgakove" (On M. A. Bulgakov), *Vospominaniia s kommentariiami* (Memoirs with commentaries) (Moscow, 1982), 392.

30. Aleksei Faiko, "Zapiski starogo teatral'shchika" (Notes of an old theaterlover), *Teatr* (Theater), no. 6 (1975):143.

31. Chudakova, "Arkhiv Bulgakova" (The Bulgakov archive), 140.

Chapter Two

1. *Zapiski iunogo vracha (A Country Doctor's Notebook);* "Polotentse s petukhom" (The towel with a cockerel), in *Izbrannaia proza* (Selected prose) (Moscow, 1966), 58.

2. Ibid.: "V'iuga" (The blizzard), 77, 81.

3. Ibid., 87.

4. Ibid.: "T'ma egipetskaia" (Egyptian darkness), 96.

5. "Zvezdnaia syp'" ("Starry Rash"), in *Meditsinskii rabotnik* (Medical worker), 12 and 19 August 1926. Michael Glenny included this story in his translation of the country doctor's notes, placing it between "Kreshchenie povorotom" (Baptism by rotation) and "The Blizzard," where it belongs chronologically. See Mikhail Bulgakov, *A Country Doctor's Notebook* (London, 1975), 61–79.

6. "Morfii" (Morphine). First published in *Meditsinskii rabotnik* (Medical worker) for 9, 17, and 23 December 1927; also published by *Russkaia mysl'* (Russian thought) in Paris, 12, 19, 26 March and 7 April 1970, and in *Literaturnaia Rossiia* (Literary Russia) (Moscow), 12 May 1978. The two texts differ slightly. I quote here from *Literaturnaia Rossiia,* 12–15. "Morphine" has been translated into English by Robert Daglish, with an introduction by Konstantin Simonov, in *Soviet Literature* (Moscow), no. 1 (1979):100–123.

7. See Vladimir Lakshin, "O proze Mikhaila Bulgakova i o nem samom" (On Bulgakov's prose and on him himself), in M. Bulgakov, *Izbrannaia proza* (Selected prose) 26; Michael Glenny, introduction to *A Country Doctor's Notebook,* by M. Bulgakov (London, 1975), x; and A. Colin Wright, *Mikhail Bulgakov: Life and Interpretations* (Toronto, 1978), 10.

8. "Neobyknovennye prikliucheniia doktora" (The extraordinary adventures of a doctor), published with an introduction by Vera Chebotareva in *Literaturnaia Gruziia* (Literary Georgia), no. 2 (1975):40.

9. See Devlet Gireev, *Mikhail Bulgakov na beregakh Tereka* (Bulgakov on the shores of the Terek River) (Ordzhonikidze, 1980), 137.

10. *Zapiski na manzhetakh* (Notes on the cuffs), published in (1) *Nakanune* (On the eve), Literary supp., 18 June 1922, 5–7; (2) *Rossiia* (Russia), no. 5 (May 1923):20–25; (3) *Vozrozhdenie* (Renaissance) (Moscow), no. 2 (1923):5–19; (4) *Zvezda vostoka* (Star of the east) (Tashkent), no. 3 (1967):11–18, with an introduction by A. Vulis; (5) *Grani* (Facets) (Frankfurt am Main), no. 77 (1970):74–81 (reprinted from *Zvezda vostoka*); (6) Texts from *Nakanune, Vozrozhdenie,* and *Rossiia* were reprinted by V. Levin in his collection of Bulgakov's works published in *Nakanune.* Levin used the incorrect title *Ranniaia neizdannaia proza* (Early unpublished prose) (Munich, 1976), 11–22, 199–212. Levin added a brief comparison of the *Nakanune* and *Vozrozhdenie* texts, which differ slightly (197–98).

11. "Mne prisnilsia son" (I dreamed a dream), published by Lidiia Ianovskaia in *Nedelia* (Week) (Moscow), no. 43 (1974):11.

12. *Zapiski na manzhetakh* (Notes on the cuffs), *Vozrozhdenie* (Renaissance) (Moscow), no. 2 (1923):7.

13. "Iz *Zapisok na manzhetakh*" (From *Notes on the Cuffs*), *Zvezda vostoka* (Star of the east) (Tashkent), no. 3 (1967):15.

14. *Vozrozhdenie* (Renaissance), 18.

15. Ibid., 19; *Nakanune* (On the eve), 7.

16. "Bogema" (Bohème), *Krasnaia niva* (Red cornfield), no. 1 (January 1925):9–13. *Krasnaia niva* is now quite rare. The Soviet scholar Lidiia Ianovskaia republished two excerpts from this story in *Avrora* (Aurora) (Msocow), no. 4 (1979):113–16, but omitted the first half of chapter 1 as well as a paragraph at the end of this chapter.

17. "Sorok sorokov. Panorama pervaia. Golye vremena" (Forty times forty. First panorama. Naked times), *Nakanune* (On the eve), 15 April 1923, 2.

18. "Moskva dvadtsatykh godov: Vstuplenie" (Moscow in the twenties: introduction), *Nakanune* (On the eve), 27 May 1924, 2.

19. "Putevye zametki" (Travel notes), *Nakanune* [On the eve], 25 May 1923.

20. "Kiev-gorod (The city of Kiev), *Nakanune* (On the eve), 6 July 1923.

21. Chudakova, "Arkhiv M. A. Bulgakova" (The Bulgakov archive), 122. The original manuscript of the preface was dated 26 November 1936, by Bulgakov. See also 81–82.

22. "Mne prisnilsia son" (I dreamed a dream), *Nedelia* (Week), no. 43 (1974):10.

23. *Teatral'nyi roman* (Theatrical novel), in *Izbrannaia proza* (Selected prose) 508.

24. Ibid., 642.

25. Yuri Slyozkin's novel *Devushka s gor* (A girl from the mountains) (Moscow, 1925) is also known under its first title, *Stolovaia gora* (Table mountain), the mountain at the foot of which Vladikavkaz is located. The hero of this novel—Alexei Vasil'evich, formerly a physician and later a writer—was modeled on Bulgakov. Valentin Kataev's short story "Zimoi" (In winter) was published several times. It first appeared in *Nakanune* (On the eve) for 15 April 1923 under the title "Pechatnyi list o sebe" (A printer's sheet about myself). Here Kataev described the story of his romance with Bulgakov's sister Elena, ridiculing Bulgakov for opposing their marriage. The story is published also in Valentin Kataev, *Sobranie sochinenii* (Collected works) (Moscow: Khudozhestvennaia literatura, 1968), 1:282–301.

26. *Teatral'nyi roman* (Theatrical novel), 543.

27. Ibid., 638.

28. Fedor Mikhalskii, *Dni i liudi Khudozhestvennogo teatra* (The people and times of the Art Theater) (Moscow: Moskovskii rabochii, 1966), 39, 44.

29. *Teatral'nyi roman,* 619.

30. Ibid., 549.

31. For a more detailed analysis see Nadine Natov, "Theatrical Novel: Bulgakov's Tragicomic Vision of His Theatrical Career," *Canadian-American Slavic Studies* 15, nos. 2–3 (Summer-Fall 1981):192–215.

32. Michael Glenny, "About Mikhail Bulgakov, His Novel, the Moscow Art Theater and Stanislavsky," in *Black Snow: A Theatrical Novel,* by Mikhail Bulgakov (Harmondsworth, 1971), 12.

33. V. Toporkov, "O 'Teatral'nom romane' Mikhaila Bulgakova" (On Mikhail Bulgakov's *Theatrical Novel*), *Novyi mir* (New world), no. 8 (1965):98.

Chapter Three

1. The stories involved here include "Ploshchad' na kolesakh" (Living quarters on wheels) in *Rasskazy* (Stories), published in 1926 in Leningrad by the publishers of the humor magazine *Smekhach* (Laughador), 51–54. See also "Tri vida svinstva" (Three kinds of swinishness), *Krasnyi perets* (Red pepper), no. 21 (1924); "Po povodu bit'ia zhen" (Concerning

124 MIKHAIL BULGAKOV

wife-beating), *Gudok* (Whistle), 18 July 1925; "O pol'ze alkogolizma" (On the usefulness of alcoholism), *Gudok* (Whistle), 15 April 1925; "Spiriticheskii seans" (Spiritualistic seance), *Rupor* (Megaphone), no. 4 (1922); "Bespokoinaia poezdka" (A troubled trip), *Gudok* (Whistle), 17 November 1923; "Nesgoraemyi amerikanskii dom" (Fireproof American house), in *Rasskazy* (Stories), 15–18; "Tipazh" (A character), *Literaturnaia gazeta* (Literary gazette), 21 February 1973; "Nedelia prosveshcheniia" (A week of enlightenment), in the Vladikavkaz newspaper *Kommunist* (Communist), April 1921; "Prosveshchenie s krovoprolitiem" (Enlightenment with bloodshed), *Gudok* (Whistle), 29 March 1924; "Lestnitsa v rai" (Staircase to paradise), *Gudok* (Whistle), 12 December 1923; "Oni khochut svoiu obrazovannost' pokazat' . . ." (They want to show their erudition), *Gudok* (Whistle), 15 February 1925; "Prikliucheniia pokoinika" (Adventures of a dead man), *Gudok* (Whistle), 27 June 1924; and "Letuchii gollandets" (Flying Dutchman), *Gudok* (Whistle), 2 September 1925.

2. For example "Biblifetchik" (Librarian-barman), *Gudok* (Whistle), 7 November 1924; "Konduktor i chlen Imperatorskoi familii" (The conductor and a member of the imperial family), *Gudok* (Whistle), 27 February 1925; "Lzhedimitrii Lunacharskii" (False Dimitry Lunacharsky), in *Rasskazy*, 18–23.

3. "Moskva krasnokamennaia" (Red-stoned Moscow), *Nakanune* (On the eve), 30 July 1922.

4. *Moskva 20-kh godov* (Moscow in the twenties), *Nakanune* (On the eve), 27 May 1924 (reprinted under the title *Traktat o zhilishche* (A treatise on housing), in a short-story collection of the same title published in 1926 in Moscow. Second chapter, "O khoroshei zhizni" (On the good life), *Nakanune* (On the eve), 12 June 1924. "Moskovskie stseny" (Moscow scenes), *Nakanune* (On the eve), Literary supp., 6 May 1923; reprinted under the title "Chetyre portreta" (Four portraits) in the collection cited above, *Traktat o zhilishche* (A treatise on housing) (Moscow: Zemlia i fabrika, 1926).

5. *Sorok sorokov* (Forty times forty), *Nakanune* (On the eve), 15 April 1923; "Pod stekliannym nebom" (Under the glassy sky), *Nakanune* (On the eve), 24 April 1923; *Stolitsa v bloknote* (The capital in a notebook), *Nakanune* (On the eve), 21 December 1922 (chaps. 1–2); 20 January 1923 (chaps. 3–4); 9 February 1923 (chaps. 5–7); 3 March 1923 (chaps. 8–10).

6. "Pokhozhdeniia Chichikova" (Chichikov's adventures), *Diavoliada: Rasskazy* (Diaboliad: stories) (Moscow, 1925), 147–60. The text consists of ten short chapters with a prologue and an epilogue. In his translation into English, Carl Proffer corrected the subtitle by defining it as a "Poem in Ten Items . . .": see "The Adventures of Chichikov," in

Diaboliad and Other Stories, ed. Ellendea Proffer and Carl Proffer (Bloomington, 1972), 159–74.

7. *Zapiski na manzhetakh* (Notes on the cuffs), *Rossiia* (Russia), no. 5 (May 1923):20–25.

8. *Diavoliada: Rasskazy* (Diaboliad: stories), 3.

9. Ibid., 42.

10. "Rokovye iaitsa" ("The Fatal Eggs") was first published in the magazine *Nedra* (Depths), no. 6 (February 1925). It was also included in the collection of stories *Diavoliada* (Diaboliad), 44–124. All page references given in parentheses in the text are to this edition. "The Fatal Eggs" was reprinted in a collection of four stories in Riga (Literatura, 1928), and in New York: *Sbornik rasskazov* (Collection of stories) (Izdatel'stvo im. Chekhova, 1952), 3–104.

11. A comparison of several of Bulgakov's works with H. G. Wells's science fiction has been done by Christine Rydel in "Bulgakov and H. G. Wells," *Russian Literature Triquarterly,* no. 15 (1978):293–311. The two authors' works display certain common features, but one should not exaggerate the Wellsian influence on Bulgakov.

12. Liubov' Belozerskaia-Bulgakova, *O, med vospominanii* (Oh, sweet reminiscences) 11, 22.

13. See, for example, A. Voronskii, "Pisatel', kniga, chitatel' " (Writer, book, and reader), *Krasnaia nov'* (Red virgin soil), no. 1 (1927):237–38; V. Pravdukhin, "*Nedra, kn. 6*" (Issue 6 of *The Depths*), *Krasnaia nov'* (Red virgin soil), no. 3 (1925):289. See L. F. Ershov, *Sovetskaia satiricheskaia proza 20-kh godov* (Soviet satirical prose of the 1920s) (Moscow: Akademiia nauk SSSR, 1960), 213–14.

14. See Sigrid McLaughlin's "Structure and Meaning in Bulgakov's 'The Fatal Eggs'," *Russian Literature Triquarterly,* no. 15 (1978):263–79. Earlier the Soviet critic Oleg Mikhailov had indicated that "The Fatal Eggs" is much more than a satire and contains an important warning concerning experiments: "Proza Bulgakova" (Bulgakov's prose), *Sibirskie ogni* (Siberian flames), no. 9 (1967):185.

15. *Sobach'e serdtse (Heart of a Dog),* first published in the magazine *Grani* (Facets) (Frankfurt am Main), no. 69 (1968):3–85; and also in *Student* (London), nos. 9–10 (1968), as well as in book form: *Sobach'e serdtse* (Paris, 1969). References in the text are to this edition. The story has been translated into many languages. See Liubov' Belozerskaia-Bulgakova, *O, med vospominanii* (Oh, sweet reminiscences), 28–29.

16. Ibid., 21, 23, 25.

17. See also Volker Levin, *Das Groteske in Michail Bulgakovs Prosa* (The grotesque in Mikhail Bulgakov's prose) (Munich, 1975), especially 32–40.

18. See, for example, the interesting discussion of both "The Fatal Eggs" and *Heart of a Dog* in Eridano Bazzarelli's *Invito alla Lettura di Bulgakov* (Introduction to Bulgakov) (Milan, 1976), 72–80. Also Helena Goscilo, "Point of View in Bulgakov's 'Heart of a Dog,' " *Russian Literature Triquarterly*, no. 15 (1978):281–91; and Diana Burgin, "Bulgakov's Early Tragedy of the Scientist-Creator: An Interpretation of 'The Heart of a Dog,' " *Slavic and East European Journal* 22, no. 4 (1978):494–508.

19. "No. 13. Dom Elpit-Rabkommuna" [Number 13. Elpit House-workers' commune] (the last name Elpit is a transformation of a real owner's name, Pigit). First publication in *Krasnyi zhurnal dlia vsekh* (Red journal for all), no. 2 (1922):23–27. Reprinted in *Diavoliada* (Diaboliad), 125–34. The quotation is from 127.

20. "Khanskii ogon' " (Khan's fire), first publication in *Krasnyi zhurnal dlia vsekh* (Red journal for all), no. 2 (1924); reprinted in *Nash sovremennik* (Our contemporary), no. 2 (1974):114–24, with an afterword by Lidiia Ianovskaia.

21. "Krasnaia korona" (Red crown), *Nakanune* (On the eve), Literary supp., 22 October 1922, 2; reprinted in *Avrora* (Aurora), no. 6 (1977), with comment by Lidiia Ianovskaia.

22. "V noch' na 3-'e chislo (Iz romana Alyi Makh)" (On the night of the third [From the novel *The Scarlet Stroke*]), *Nakanune* (On the eve), literary supp., 10 December 1922. This novel was never finished. Some ideas, situations, and protagonists resemble those found in *The White Guard,* but the basic structure is different.

23. "Nalet (V volshebnom fonare)" (The Raid [In a magic lantern]), signed with the initials M. B., *Gudok* (Whistle), 25 December 1923. Reprinted in *Ranniaia nesobrannaia proza,* ed. Volker Levin (Munich, 1978), 182–88. Also reprinted in the Soviet Union by Lidiia Ianovskaia with an afterword: see *Avrora* (Aurora), no. 4 (1982):95–102.

24. "Ia ubil" (I Killed), *Meditsinskii rabotnik* (Medical worker), 18 November 1926, 13–15, and 12 December 1926, 14–16. Reprinted in *Nedelia* (Week), no. 14 (1972):6–7.

Chapter Four

1. "Kiev-gorod" (The city of Kiev), *Nakanune* (On the eve), 6 July 1923, 2–4.

2. "Avtobiografiia" (Autobiography), in *Sovetskie pisateli: Avtobiografii,* 3:86. Isai Lezhnev published only the first two parts of the novel. When the Riga publishing house Literaturnaia Riga (Literary Riga) issued it in 1927, the third part was not written by Bulgakov. The first two parts were taken from *Rossiia* (Russia), with a few arbitrary changes; while the third part was compiled by the editors on the basis of one of the two

earlier versions of the play *Days of the Turbins*. The hoax was pointed out by the Concorde publishing house in Paris, which issued the full text of the novel in two volumes: the first in 1927, the second in 1929, with the double title *Dni Turbinykh (Belaia guardiia) (The Days of the Turbins [The White Guard])* and the notation "Copyright 1929 by the author." The Concorde publishers emphasized the authenticity of their text, which was published with Bulgakov's authorization.

3. Historical data have been taken from the following sources: *Entsiklopediia Ukrainoznavstva* (Encyclopedia of the Ukraine), ed. V. Kubievich (Munich: Shevchenko Scientific Society, 1949), 2:512; Peter Kenez, *Civil War in South Russia, 1918* (Berkeley: University of California Press, 1971); *Istoriia Kommunisticheskoi partii Sovetskogo Soiuza* (History of the Communist party of the Soviet Union) (Moscow: Politicheskaia literatura, 1969).

4. *Belaia gvardiia: Izbrannaia proza* (The White Guard: selected prose) 113. All references to *The White Guard* in the text are to this edition.

5. Ezra, 3:1, 5; Rev. 8–9.

6. Elena's vision anticipates ideas and landscapes that will recur a few years later in the "ancient" chapters of *The Master and Margarita*.

7. The most extensive and comprehensive analysis of the novel has been done by an Italian scholar: Leone Pacini Savoj, "La 'Guardia Bianca' di M. A. Bulgakov" (Bulgakov's *White Guard*), in *Saggi di letturatura russa* (Essays on Russian literature) (Florence: Sansoni, 1978), 139–260.

8. The passage about the magic box is from *Teatral'nyi roman* (Theatrical novel), in Bulgakov's *Izbrannaia proza* (Selected prose), 538–39. Elena Poliakova referred to this as a passage from "one of Bulgakov's unpublished novels" in her book *Teatr i dramaturgiia* (Theater and drama) (Moscow: Vserossiiskoe teatral'noe obshchestvo, 1959), 38–39. A detailed analysis of the play's genesis has been done by Iakov Lur'e and Il'ia Serman in "Ot 'Beloi gvardii' k 'Dniam Turbinykh' " (From *The White Guard* to *The Days of the Turbins*), *Russkaia literatura* (Russian literature), no. 2 (1965):194–203. See also Vera Chebotareva's article "K istorii sozdaniia 'Beloi gvardii' " (On the history of the creation of *The White Guard*), *Russkaia literatura* (Russian literature), no. 4 (1974):148–52.

9. E. I. Poliakova speaks of the long process of reworking the first version of the stage adaptation of the novel into a play (*Teatr i dramaturgiia*, 42). In his introduction to the 1962 edition of Bulgakov's plays Pavel Markov refers to the first version of Bulgakov's manuscript as a stage adaptation, but then states that, in its final version, the play became a "completely independent work" for which the novel was only a point of departure, a source: Pavel Markov, "Bulgakov," in *P'esy* (Plays), by M. Bulgakov, 9–10.

10. Il'ia Sudakov, "Rannie roli N. P. Khmeleva" (N. P. Khmelev's early roles), *Ezhegodnik MKhATa* (Yearbook of the Moscow Art Theater) (Moscow: Iskusstvo, 1948), 2:38.

11. See Chudakova, "Arkhiv M. A. Bulgakova" (The Bulgakov archive), notes on 58–59.

12. K. Rudnitskii, "Vozvrashchenie Turbinykh" (The return of the Turbins), *Vecherniaia Moskva* (Evening Moscow), 1 February 1968.

13. *Dni Turbinykh (Days of the Turbins)*, in *P'esy* (Plays), 84.

14. Vladimir Nemirovich-Danchenko, in the newspaper *Gorkovets* (Gorkyite), 15 February 1934.

15. Konstantin Rudnitskii, "Bulgakov," *Spektakli raznykh let* (Performances of various years) (Moscow: Iskusstvo, 1974), 240. The first part of this long article is an expanded version of Rudnitskii's review cited above, note 12.

16. General Baron P. N. Wrangel, *Vospominanii* (Memoirs), edited by A. A. von Lampe (Frankfurt am Main: Possev, 1969), p. 2, 235.

17. Richard Luckett, *The White Generals: An Account of the White Movement and the Russian Civil War* (New York: Viking Press, 1971), 384. See also Peter Kenez, *Civil War in South Russia 1919–1920* (Berkeley: University of California Press, 1977), chapter on Wrangel.

18. Apparently here Bulgakov was describing the actual situation at the important Taganash railroad station, which was blocked at that time by several military trains because of the unusual cold and the retreat of the White troops after the decisive battles waged on 5–7 November at the Taganash Isthmus on the Chongar peninsula.

19. *Beg (Flight)*, in *P'esy* (Plays) (1962), 214. References in the text are to this edition.

20. *Teatr* (Theater) (Moscow), no. 9 (1969):120. The first production of *Flight* took place at the Gorky Drama Theater in Volgograd (formerly Stalingrad) in 1957, and broke a thirty-year silence. The prestigious Pushkin Drama Theater in Leningrad then premiered it on 27 June 1958. It was staged at the Chamber Theater in Prague in 1959, and at the Polish Theater in Bygdoszcz, Poland, in 1960. In 1967 it was produced at the Ermolova Theater in Moscow by Andrei Goncharov, who later produced it at the National Theater in Sofia, Bulgaria, and, in 1978, at the Mayakovsky Theater in Moscow. In that same year it was staged at the Theater of Satire in Moscow as well.

21. Ellendea Proffer, introduction to *Flight* in *The Early Plays of Mikhail Bulgakov* (Bloomington, 1972), 163–64.

22. Mirra Ginsburg, introduction to *Flight*, by M. Bulgakov (New York: Grove Press, 1969), 9. See also Barbara Kejna Sharratt, "*Flight*: A Symphonic Play," *Canadian Slavonic Papers* 14, no. 1 (1972):79.

Chapter Five

1. Liubov' Belozerskaia-Bulgakova, *O, med vospominanii* (Oh sweet reminiscences), 29.

2. *Teatral'nyi roman* (Theatrical novel), in *Izbrannaia proza* (Selected prose), 619. See also *Black Snow: A Theatrical Novel,* trans. Michael Glenny (Harmondsworth, 1971), 157–58.

3. There are now two text versions of the play *Zoikina kvartira:* one written by Bulgakov in 1925 and produced by the Vakhtangov Theater for 2½ years; and a corrected version, marked "final text," written by Bulgakov in 1935. Bulgakov defined the final text as a "tragic farce." The differences in the content and plot of the two versions are not major. The first version was published in *Novyi zhurnal* (New review) (New York), no. 97 (1969) and no. 98 (1970); the second version was published in Bulgakov's *P'esy* (Plays) (Paris, 1971). It was earlier published in English, with commentary, by Carl and Ellendea Proffer: "Zoia's Apartment," *Canadian Slavic Studies* (Montreal) 4, no. 2 (Summer 1970):238–87.

4. *Novyi zhurnal,* no. 97 (1969):70; *P'esy,* 204.

5. The Soviet scholar Dmitrii Likhachev regarded Ametistov as a Russian version of Alfred Gingle from Charles Dickens's *Pickwick Papers.* See D. S. Likhachev, "Literaturnyi ded Ostapa Bendera" (A literary ancestor of Ostap Bender), in *Stranitsy istorii russkoi literatury* (Pages from the history of Russian literature) (Moscow: Nauka, 1971), 245–48. Ostap Bender is the protagonist of two famous humorous novels by Il'ia Il'f and Evgenii Petrov.

6. Aleksei Popov, "Vospominaniia i razmyshleniia" (Reminiscences and meditations), *Teatr* (Theater), no. 5 (1960):118.

7. Bulgakov's *Bagrovyi ostrov (The Crimson Island)* has never been published in the Soviet Union. The Russian text (prologue and acts 1–2) was first published in *Novyi zhurnal* (New review) (New York), no. 93 (1968):38–76; and the complete text by YMCA Press in *P'esy* (Plays). (1971). Carl and Ellendea Proffer translated the play into English and published it in *The Early Plays of Mikhail Bulgakov.*

8. A detailed analysis of the play's structure has been done by the German scholar Herta Schmid in her article "Das Verfahren des Illusionsbruchs in Bulgakovs *Bagrovyj ostrov*" (The handling of the destruction of illusions in Bulgakov's *Crimson Island*), *Canadian-American Slavic Studies* 15, nos. 2–3 (Summer-Fall 1981):216–37.

9. *Bagrovyi ostrov* (The Crimson Island), in *P'esy* (Plays), (1971), 181.

10. Other heroes from Jules Verne also appear. Glenarvan's romantic Captain John Mangles gives place in Bulgakov's play to Captain Hatteras (from *Les Aventures du Capitaine Hatteras* [The adventures of Captain Hatteras, 1866]), whose gloomy nature is changed to the boisterous high

spirits of a pirate. The absent-minded Jacques Paganel, Glenarvan's loyal companion and an honorable member of the French Geographic Society, is also transformed into a jovial "French imperialist" who goes halves with the lord in buying the natives' pearls. Paganel's servant Passepartout comes from *Le Tour du Monde en quatre-vingts jours* (*Around the World in Eighty Days*, 1873), where he, a French ex-acrobat, serves and accompanies the British clubman Phileas Fogg on his tour. Even the Maoris who hold Paganel in captivity are changed into "positive" Red native leaders Kai-Kum and Farra-Tété.

11. Liubov' Belozerskaia-Bulgakova, *O, med vospominanii* (Oh sweet reminiscences), 59. The author also points out that the fight between the white and red Moors at the Crimson Island is merely a humorous background, "only foam, laces." The essence of the play is the fate of a young writer and his dependence on an "ominous old man," the censor Savva Lukich.

12. *Bagrovyi ostrov* (The crimson island), 183–84.

13. Ibid., 90. Nikolai Gogol', *Revizor (The Inspector General)*, act 1, scene 1.

14. E. S-oi, "Ubogoe zrelishche (na spektakle 'Bagrovyi ostrov')" (A pitiful spectacle [at a performance of *The Crimson Island*]), *Trud* (Labor), 29 December 1928.

15. B. Miliavskii, *Satirik i vremia* (The satirist and time) (Moscow: Sovetskii pisatel', 1963), 245–46.

16. The corrected version of the play was published by YMCA Press in Paris in *P'esy* (Plays), (1971), 5–77. Page references in the text are to this edition. Ellendea Proffer has translated an earlier version into English: *Adam and Eve*, in *Russian Literature Triquarterly*, no. 1 (1971):165–215.

17. The content of *Adam and Eve* was briefly summarized by V. A. Sakhnovskii-Pankeev in "Bulgakov," *Ocherki istorii ruskoi sovetskoi dramaturgii* (Essays in the history of Soviet Russian drama) (Moscow: Iskusstvo, 1966), 2:134–35.

18. Christine Rydel discovers in *Adam and Eve* certain echoes of H. G. Wells's views on the future as expounded in *The World Set Free* and *The Autocracy of Mr. Parham*. See her article "Bulgakov and H. G. Wells," 303–5.

19. A. Colin Wright, who has done a fine detailed analysis of *Adam and Eve*, considers it "the most intellectual and literary of Bulgakov's plays," "all too relevant to today's age." See his *Mikhail Bulgakov: Life and Interpretation*, 161.

20. *Blazhenstvo (Son inzhenera Reina v 4-kh deistviiakh)* (Bliss [A dream of Engineer Rein in four acts]), *Zvezda vostoka* (Star of the east), no. 7 (1966):75–107. Page references in the text are to this periodical. The play

was reprinted in *Grani* (Facets) (Frankfurt am Main), no. 85 (1972):3–52.

21. Here Bulgakov jokingly uses the name of the protagonist of the popular historical novel by the same title by Mikhail Zagoskin, published in 1829.

22. "Bulgakov," in *Sovetskie pisateli: Avtobiografii* (Soviet writers: autobiographies) 3:99.

23. *Ivan Vasil'evich,* a comedy in three acts. First published in *Ivan Vasil'evich. Mertvye dushi* (Ivan Vasil'evich. Dead Souls) (Munich: Tovarishchestvo zarubezhnykh pisatelei, 1964), 7–70. A year later it was publilshed in *Dramy i komedii* (Dramas and comedies) 413–74. References given in the text are to this edition.

24. The production at the Movie Actor Theater was reviewed by Konstantin Rudnitskii: see his chapter "Bulgakov" in *Spektakli raznykh let* (Performances of various years), 258–63. Rudnitskii criticizes the exaggeration of its grotesque features: in this Vuros production Bulgakov's fine humor was often replaced by jokes and pranks. The approach of the Drama Theater in Irkutsk, where Bulgakov's comedy was performed in 1965–66, was not much better: see the review by B. Smelkov, "Piat' sezonov Irkutskogo teatra" (Five seasons of Irkutsk theater), *Teatr* (Theater), no. 10 (1969):58. T. Sukhanova praised the 1979 production of *Ivan Vasil'evich* by A. Kuznetsov at the Drama Theater in Smolensk as a hilarious comedy full of wit and humor: "Ivan Vasil'evich ne meniaet professiiu" (Ivan Vasil'evich does not change his profession), *Teatr* (Theater), no. 8 (1979):29–33. The movie director Leonid Gaidai in 1971 produced a comedy entitled *Ivan Vasil'evich Changes Profession.* Press reaction was mixed.

25. See Igor' Savich (director of the play), "K postanovke 'Blazhenstva' M. A. Bulgakova" (On the staging of Bulgakov's *Bliss*), *Russkaia mysl'* (Russian thought), 11 May 1978.

Chapter Six

1. *Teatral'nyi roman* (Theatrical novel), in *Izbrannaia proza* (Selected prose) 619.

2. Molière used the name Brindavoine for one of Harpagon's two lackeys in *L'Avare* (*The Miser,* 1668), which Bulgakov translated into Russian in 1936. In *A Cabal of Hypocrites* Molière's servant is named Bouton.

3. *Poloumnyi Zhurden: Molieriana v trekh deistviiakh* (Half-witted Jourdain: Molièriana in three acts), in *Dramy i komedii* (Dramas and comedies) 303–4.

4. Ibid., 337.

5. *Kabala sviatosh* (A cabal of hypocrites), *P'esy* (Plays), 269.

6. Ibid., 273.

7. Ibid., 284.

8. K. Rudnitskii, "Molier, 'Tartuf' i Bulgakov" (Molière, *Tartuffe,* and Bulgakov), *Nauka i religiia* (Science and religion), no. 1 (1972):88.

9. J.-L. Le Gallois, Sieur de Grimarest, *La Vie de Mr. de Molière* (The life of Molière) (Paris: Isidore Liseux; 1877); first published in 1705.

10. *Zhizn' gospodina de Moliera* (Life of Monsieur de Molière) (Moscow, 1962), 97. All page citations given in the text are to this edition. The novel was reprinted in Bulgakov's *Izbrannaia proza* (Selected prose), 349–504. English translations are taken mostly from *The Life of Monsieur de Molière,* trans. Mirra Ginsburg (New York, 1970).

11. On this point Bulgakov remained closer to historical fact than did his critics who accused him of falsifying Molière's biography and neglecting his social milieu. See, for example, the unsigned article "Vneshnii blesk i fal'shivoe soderzhanie" (Outward brilliance and false content) in *Pravda* (Truth) for 9 March 1936; and G. Boiadzhiev, "Kratkoe preduvedomlenie" (Brief preamble), in Bulgakov's *Zhizn' gospodina de Moliera* (Life of Monsieur de Molière) 6.

12. Pierre Roullé, "Le Roi Glorieux au Monde ou Louis XIV Le Plus Glorieux de Tous Les Rois du Monde" (The king glorious in the world, or Louis XIV, the most glorious of all kings in the world). The full text of this panegryic of 1664 was published by Georges Mongrédien, *Recueil des Textes et des Documents du XVIIe siècle relatifs à Molière* (Anthology of texts and documents of the 17th century on Molière), vol. 1 (Paris: Centre National de la Recherche Scientifique, 1965). The quotation is from 220.

13. J. D. Hubert, *Molière and the Comedy of Intellect* (Berkeley: University of California Press, 1962), 266.

14. The famous Fontaine de Molière was erected at the intersection of rue de Richelieu, rue de Molière, and rue Thérèse. Bulgakov asked his brother in Paris to send him a detailed description of the monument.

15. Bulgakov's manuscript, dated "Moscow, 1932–33," was rejected, and the Editorial Committee commissioned a more "suitable" biography from Stefan Mokulskii, a historian of literature and the theater with a specialty in French literature and drama of the seventeenth and eighteenth centuries. His book came out in 1936. Only in 1962 was it recognized that Bulgakov "preserves the artistic and psychological truth which helps him to understand the historical truth" (V. Lakshin, "Dve biografii" [Two biographies], *Novyi mir* [New world], no. 3 [1963]:254). The writer Valentin Kaverin completed his afterword to the first edition of Bulgakov's novel with the comment that it would take an "important place" in the series of biographies which Maksim Gorky had instituted: see Bulgakov's *Zhizn' gospodina de Moliere* (Life of Monsieur de Molière), 232. And A. Colin Wright has written: "It is this picture of Molière as an ordinary person which Bulgakov contrasts with the immortality of his

works"; and he terms Bulgakov's novel "a remarkable book, whose subject provides universal interest" (*Mikhail Bulgakov: Life and Interpretations,* 183, 185). Wright is certainly correct; in particular, the book's peculiar structure deserves more analysis than it has received to this point.

Chapter Seven

1. Chudakova, "Tvorcheskaia istoriia romana M. Bulgakova 'Master i Margarita' " (The creative history of Bulgakov's *Master and Margarita*), *Voprosy literatury* (Problems of literature), no. 1 (1976):218–53. See the English translation "*The Master and Margarita:* The Development of a Novel," *Russian Literature Triquarterly,* no. 15 (1978):177–209.

2. See Ellendea Proffer, "On *The Master and Margarita,*" *Russian Literature Triquarterly,* no. 6 (1973):533–64; Barbara Kejna Sharratt, "Narrative Techniques in *The Master and Margarita,*" *Canadian Slavonic Papers* 16, no. 1 (1974):1–12; Heinrich Riggenbach, *Michail Bulgakovs Roman "Master i Margarita": Stil und Gestalt* (Bulgakov's novel *Master and Margarita:* style and form) (Bern, 1979), 131–80; and Vida Taranovski Johnson, "The Thematic Function of the Narrator in *The Master and Margarita,*" *Canadian-American Slavic Studies* 15, nos. 2–3 (1981):271–86.

3. *Master i Margarita,* in *Romany* (Novels) (Moscow, 1973). All page references to *The Master and Margarita* in the text are to this edition.

4. Chudakova, "Arkhiv M. A. Bulgakova" (The Bulgakov archive) 70.

5. At Walpurgisnacht Mephistopheles called himself "Junker Voland" when he led Faust out from the crowd of witches seeking to separate them (*Faust,* pt. 2, vv. 4021–25).

6. The affinities, as well as differences, with *Faust* are significant and complex, and have already received much attention in Bulgakov criticism. The most detailed study of the question has been done by Elizabeth Stenbock-Fermor in her "Bulgakov's *The Master and Margarita* and Goethe's *Faust,*" *Slavic and East European Journal* 13, no. 3 (1969), esp. 309–16. But there are a number of other works on the same topic: V. Lakshin, "Roman M. Bulgakova 'Master i Margarita' " (Bulgakov's *The Master and Margarita*), *Novyi mir* (New world), no. 6, (1968), esp. 292–95; A. Colin Wright, "Satan in Moscow," *PMLA* 88, no. 5 (October 1973), esp. 1162–68; Edith Haber, "The Mythic Structure of Bulgakov's *The Master and Margarita,*" *Russian Review* 34, no. 4 (October 1975):382–409; Nadine Natov, "Structural and Typological Ambivalence of Bulgakov's Novels Interpreted Against the Background of Bakhtin's Theory of 'Grotesque Realism' and Carnivalization," *American Contributions to the Eighth International Congress of Slavists* (Columbus, Ohio, 1978), 2:536–49.

7. The critic Viktor Petelin emphasized the Master's courage in his article "Vozvrashchenie mastera" (The Master's return), *Moskva* (Moscow), no. 7 (1976):208–9.

8. Parallels between the Master's words and Pilate's are enumerated in Ellendea Proffer's article "Bulgakov's *The Master and Margarita:* Genre and Motif," *Canadian Slavic Studies* 3, no. 4 (Winter 1969):615–28.

9. The affinities with Dante's *Divine Comedy* have been investigated by Bruce Beatie and Phyllis Powell in their article "Bulgakov, Dante, and Relativity," *Canadian-American Slavic Studies* 15, nos. 2–3 (Summer-Fall 1981):261–67.

10. See, e.g., Heinz Zahrnt, *The Historical Jesus,* trans. J. S. Boweden (New York: Harper and Row, 1963); and Carl Braaten and Roy Harrisville, eds., *The Historical Jesus and the Kerygmatic Christ: Essays on the New Quest of the Historical Jesus* (New York: Abington Press, 1964).

11. See Albert Schweitzer, *The Quest of the Historical Jesus (A Critical Study of Its Progress from Reimarus to Wrede)* (New York: Macmillan Co., 1950); David Friedrich Strauss, *Das Leben Jesu* (The life of Jesus) (first edition 1835), or in English *The Life of Jesus Critically Examined,* trans. George Eliot (Philadlphia: Fortress Press, 1972); Ernest Renan, *Vie de Jesus* (Life of Jesus) (Paris: Calmann Levy, n.d.) (first published in 1863).

12. The Gospel of Nicodemus, formerly called The Acts of Pontius Pilate, in *The Lost Books of the Bible* (New York: Bell, 1979). Consider especially the names and the behavior of the two other prisoners crucified with Jesus: 6:23, 7:3 ("And in like manner did they to the two thieves who were crucified with him, Dimas on his right hand and Gestas on his left"), and 7:10–12. The historical sources were first suggested by Rostislav Pletnev in his "Pontii Pilat i roman M. Bulgakova" (Pontius Pilate and Bulgakov's novel), *Novoe russkoe slovo* (New Russian word), 22 September 1968. Research into the sources of the Pilate-Yeshua chapters began only a few years ago. Among works in which this problem is discussed at length should be mentioned the book by Henrikh Elbaum, *Analiz iudeiskikh glav Mastera i Margarity M. Bulgakova* (An analysis of the Judaic chapters of Bulgakov's *The Master and Margarita*) (Ann Arbor: Ardis, 1981).

13. See Tacitus's *Annals* in *The Complete Works* (New York: Random House, 1942), bk. 6, 29–51.

14. St. John records that Jesus gave the sop to Judas Iscariot: "And after the sop Satan entered into him. Then said Jesus unto him, 'That thou doest, do quickly' " (13:27).

Chapter Eight

1. Vitalii Vilenkin, "O Mikhaile Afanas'eviche Bulgakove" (On M. A. Bulgakov), in *Vospominaniia s kommentariiami* (Reminiscences with commentaries) (Moscow, 1982), 388.

2. *Poslednie dni (Pushkin) (The Last Days)*, in *P'esy* (Plays), (1962), 328–29. All page references in the text are to this edition. The play has been rendered into English by Carl Proffer in *Russian Literature Triquarterly*, no. 15 (1978):49–97.

3. M. Bulgakov and V. Veresaev, "Perepiska po povodu p'esy 'Push-kin' ('Poslednie dni')" (Correspondence concerning the play *Pushkin* [*The Last Days*]), *Voprosy literatury* (Problems of literature), no. 3 (1965):151–71. Veresaev's book was *Pushkin v zhizni* (Pushkin in life) (Moscow: Nedra, 1927).

4. Konstantin Danzas, "Poslednie dni zhizni i konchina Aleksandra Sergeevicha Pushkina" (The last days of life and the demise of A. S. Pushkin), in *Pushkin v vospominaniiakh sovremennikov* (Pushkin in the memoirs of his contemporaries) (Leningrad: Khudozhestvennaia literatura, 1950), 491–94.

5. P. A. Viazemskii, "Iz vospominanii" (From my memoirs), in ibid., 134.

6. K. Derzhavin, "Don Kikhot" (Don Quixote), *Izvestiia* (News), 20 March 1941. See also V. A. Sakhnovskii-Pankeev, "Bulgakov," in *Ocherki istorii russkoi sovetskoi dramaturgii* (Essays in the history of Soviet Russian drama) (Moscow, 1966), 2:141–42; R. Beniash, "Cherkasov," *Teatr* (Theater), no. 2 (1970):81–84; K. Rudnitskii, "Don Kikhot" (Don Quixote), in *P'esy* (Plays), by Bulgakov, (1962), 478–80. Page references in the text to the play *Don Quixote* are to this edition.

7. Wright, *Mikhail Bulgakov: Life and Interpretations*, 248.

8. M. Chudakova, "Arkhiv M. A. Bulgakova" (The Bulgakov archive), 134–35; Vitalii Vilenkin, "O Mikhaile Afanas'eviche Bulgakov" (On M. A. Bulgakov), 395–96.

9. *Batum*, in *Neizdannyi Bulgakov: Teksty i materialy* (Unpublished Bulgakov: texts and materials), 160.

10. The text of the play *Mertvye dushi* (Dead Souls) was published in *Ivan Vasil'evich. Mertvye dushi*, 71–145. The filmscript for *Dead Souls* was published in *Moskva* (Moscow), no. 1 (1978):125–64, as M. Bulgakov and I. Pyriev, *Mertvye dushi: Kinostsenarii*. The filmscript *The Inspector General* was published in New York: "Revizor—kinostsenarii M. Bulgakova" [The inspector general—a Filmscript by Bulgakov], with an introduction by A. C. Wright, *Novyi zhurnal* (New Review), no. 127 (1977):5–45.

11. A valuable study has been published by Lesley Milne: "M. A. Bulgakov and *Dead Souls:* The Problem of Adaptation," *Slavonic and East European Review* 52, no. 128 (July 1974):420–40. See also M. Chudakova, "Bulgakov i Gogol' " (Bulgakov and Gogol), *Russkaia rech'* (Russian speech), no. 2 (1979):38–48; no. 3 (1979):55–59.

12. See B. F. Egorov, "M. A. Bulgakov—'perevodchik' Gogolia" (Bulgakov as Gogol's "translator"), in *Ezhegodnik Rukopisnogo otdela Push-*

kinskogo doma na 1976 god (Yearbook of the manuscript section of the Pushkin house for 1976) (Leningrad: Nauka, 1978), 57–84.

13. The Russian text has been published by A. C. Wright with an introduction: "Mikhail Bulgakov's Adaptation of *War and Peace*," *Canadian-American Slavic Studies* 15, nos. 2–3 (Summer-Fall 1981):382–439.

14. "Perepiska B. V. Asaf'eva s M. A. Bulgakovym" (Correspondence of B. V. Asafiev with Bulgakov), *Muzyka Rossii* (Music of Russia), no. 3 (1980):262–90.

15. See Michael Glenny, "Mikhail Bulgakov," *Survey* no. 65 (October 1967):13.

Selected Bibliography

The list of works on Bulgakov is lengthening rapidly. As the notes and references include all of Bulgakov's works and numerous books and articles on him and his writings, only the most important editions and critical works will be enumerated here.

PRIMARY SOURCES

1. Works in Russian
"Khanskii ogon'." *Krasnyi zhurnal dlia vsekh* (Moscow), no. 2 (1924). Reprinted: *Nash sovremennik* (Moscow), no. 2 (1974); 114–24, with afterword by Lidiia Ianovskaia.
Diavoliada. Moscow: Nedra, 1925. Five stories: "Diavoliada," "Rokovye iaitsa," "Nr. 13. Dom Elpit Rabkommuna," "Kitaiskaia istoriia," and "Pokhozhdeniia Chichikova."
Sobach'e serdtse. Paris: YMCA Press, 1969.
P'esy. Introduction by Pavel Markov. Moscow: Iskusstvo, 1962. Five plays: *Dni Turbinykh, Beg, Kabala sviatosh, Poslednie dni, Don Kikhot.*
Dramy i komedii. Introduction by Veniamin Kaverin. Moscow: Iskusstvo, 1965. Seven plays: Five as in *P'esy,* and *Poloumnyi Zhurden* and *Ivan Vasil'evich.*
P'esy. Paris: YMCA Press, 1971. Three plays: *Adam i Eva, Bagrovyi ostrov,* and *Zoikina kvartira.*
Izbrannaia proza. Introduction by Vladimir Lakshin. Moscow: Khudozhestvennaia literatura, 1966. Contains *Zapiski iunogo vracha, Belaia gvardiia, Zhizn' gospodina de Moliera,* and *Teatral'nyi roman.*
Romany. Introduction by Konstantin Simonov. Moscow: Khudozhestvennaia literatura, 1973. Includes *Belaia gvardiia, Teatral'nyi roman, Master i Margarita.*
Romany. Reprint (of 1973 edition). Leningrad: Khudozhestvennaia literatura, Leningradskoe otdelenie, 1978.
Master i Margarita. Ann Arbor: Ardis, 1980.
Izbrannoe. Introduction by Evgenii Sidorov; afterword "O rasskazakh" and "O romane" by Marietta Chudakova. Moscow: Khudozhestvennaia literatura, 1980. Includes *Master i Margarita* and seven short stories: "Polotentse s petukhom," "V'iuga," "T'ma egipetskaia," "Morfii," "Psalom," "Ia ubil," and "Khanskii ogon'."

Avtobiografiia. In *Sovetskie pisateli: Avtobiografii,* 3:85—87. Moscow: Khu-
    dozhestvennaia literatura, 1966.
Sobranie sochinenii. In *Collected Works,* edited by Ellendea Proffer, vol. 1.
    Introduction by E. Proffer. Ann Arbor: Ardis, 1982. Includes *Zapiski
    iunogo vracha,* stories on Civil War, *Zapiski na manzhetakh,* and stories
    from the paper *Nakanune.*
Ranniaia neizdannaia proza. Compiled, with introduction, by Volker Levin.
    Munich: Otto Sagner, 1976. The title is incorrect: the collection
    consists of Bulgakov's stories published in 1922—24 in the Berlin
    paper *Nakanune* and of passages from *Notes on the Cuffs,* published in
    the almanacs *Vozrozhdenie* and *Rossiia.*
Ranniaia nesobrannaia proza. Compiled by Volker Levin and L. V. Svetin,
    with introduction by Volker Levin. Munich: Otto Sagner, 1978.
    Contents: feuilletons and short stories of 1921—26 from Soviet Russian
    papers and magazines such as *Gudok, Krasnyi perets, Krasnyi zhurnal
    dlia vsekh, Rupor,* and *Meditsinskii rabotnik.*

2. English translations
The Master and Margarita. Translated by Mirra Ginsburg. New York:
    Grove Press, 1967 (censored version). Translated by Michael Glenny.
    London: Harvill Press, 1967 (complete version).
Heart of a Dog. Translated by Mirra Ginsburg. New York: Grove Press,
    1968. Translated by Michael Glenny as *The Heart of a Dog.* Intro-
    duction by M. Glenny. New York: Harper & Row, 1968.
Black Snow: A Theatrical Novel. Translated, with introduction, by Michael
    Glenny. Harmondsworth: Penguin Books, 1971.
Life of Monsieur de Molière. Translated by Mirra Ginsburg. New York: Funk
    & Wagnalls, 1970.
The White Guard. Translated by Michael Glenny, with "The House of the
    Turbins" by Viktor Nekrasov as afterword. New York: McGraw-
    Hill, 1971.
Diaboliad and Other Stories. Translated by Carl R. Proffer, introduction by
    Carl and Ellendea Proffer. Bloomington: Indiana University Press,
    1972. Eleven stories.
The Early Plays of Mikhail Bulgakov. Translated, with introduction, by
    Carl R. and Ellendea Proffer. Bloomington: Indiana University Press,
    1972. Five plays: *The Days of the Turbins, Zoya's Apartment, Flight,
    The Crimson Island,* and *A Cabal of Hypocrites.*
A Country Doctor's Notebook. Translated, with introduction, by Michael
    Glenny. London: Bantam Books, 1975.

SECONDARY SOURCES

Bazzarelli, Eridano. *Invito alla lettura di Bulgakov* (Introduction to the
    reading of Bulgakov). Milan: Ugo Mursia, 1976. First general survey

of Bulgakov's life and works in book form with chronology and bibliography.

Belozerskaia-Bulgakova, Liubov' E. *O, med vospominanii* (Oh sweet reminiscences). Ann Arbor: Ardis, 1979. Contains some scattered but still valuable material on Bulgakov's live in the late 1920s.

Belza, Igor'. "Genealogiia Mastera i Margarity" (The genealogy of *The Master and Margarita*). In *Kontekst—1978* (Context—1978), 156–248. Moscow: Nauka (Science), 1978. The author treats the Gospels as among the novel's sources. Contains a few questionable statements.

Burmistrov, A. S. "K biografii M. A. Bulgakova (1891–1916)" (Toward a biography of M. A. Bulgakov). In *Kontekst—1978*, 249–66. Moscow: Nauka (Science), 1978. Contains valuable information on Bulgakov's family and his youth.

Canadian-American Slavic Studies 15, nos. 2–3 (1981). Special issue edited by Nadine Natov. Thirteen articles by American and European scholars dealing with Bulgakov's craft, especially in *The Master and Margarita* and *Theatrical Novel,* Bulgakov's world view, and his biography. Also contains recent bibliography, a checklist of materials in Soviet archives, and Bulgakov's adaptation of *War and Peace*.

Chudakova, Marietta. "Arkhiv M. A. Bulgakova" (The Bulgakov archive). In *Zapiski otdela rukopisei Vsesoiuznoi biblioteki im. Lenina,* 37 (Transactions of the Manuscript Division of the All-Union Lenin Library, no. 37), 25–151. Moscow: Kniga (Book), 1976. The most important source of information on Bulgakov's life and the history of his publications.

Chudakova, Marietta. "Bulgakov i Gogol' " (Bulgakov and Gogol). *Russkaia rech'* (Russian speech) (Moscow), no. 2 (March–April 1979):38–48; no. 3 (May–June 1979):55–59. A comparative study of some themes in Bulgakov and Gogol.

Ermolinskii, Sergei A. "Mikhail Bulgakov: Iz zapisok raznykh let" (Mikhail Bulgakov: Notes of Various Years). In *Dramaticheskie sochineniia* (Dramatic works), 583–700. Moscow: Iskusstvo (Art), 1982. Useful, though sometimes too subjective, information on Bulgakov's life and environment in the 1930s.

Gasparov, Boris M. "Iz nabliudenii nad motivnoi strukturoi romana M. A. Bulgakova *Master i Margarita*" (Some remarks on the motif structure of Bulgakov's novel *The Master and Margarita*). *Slavica Hierosolymitana* (Slavic studies of the Hebrew University) (Jerusalem) 3 (1978):198–251. The author analyzes the novel as a "novel-myth," traces hidden references to the associations with other writers, literary works, and Russian folklore.

Gireev, Devlet. *Mikhail Bulgakov na beregakh Tereka* (M. Bulgakov on the shores of the Terek River). Ordzhonikidze: Ir, 1980. An attempt, in a fictionalized form based on Bulgakov's early stories and letters, to reconstruct his life in the Caucasus. Contains valuable references to Caucasian newspapers and some archival material.

An International Bibliography of Works by and about Mikhail Bulgakov. Compiled by Ellendea Proffer. Ann Arbor: Ardis, 1976.

Krugovoi, Georgii. "Gnosticheskii roman" (A gnostic novel). *Novyi zhurnal* (New review) (New York), no. 134 (1979):47–81. Interprets the novel, drawing upon a theory of Father Pavel Florensky, as an expression of various dimensions of man's spiritual world. Discusses the novel's rich symbolism.

Lakshin, Vladimir. "Roman M. Bulgakova 'Master i Margarita' " (Bulgakov's novel *The Master and Margarita*). *Novyi Mir* (New world) (Moscow), no. 6 (1968):284–311. One of the best and most detailed discussions of the novel's structure and meaning by a Soviet scholar.

Levin, Volker. *Das Groteske in Michail Bulgakovs Prosa* (The grotesque in Mikhail Bulgakov's prose). Munich: Otto Sagner, 1975. A good scholarly discussion of various aspects and functions of the grotesque in three stories and *The Master and Margarita*.

Markov, Pavel A. "Iz vospominanii: vstrechi s dramaturgami" (From my reminiscences: meetings with playwrights). In *V Khudozhestvennom teatre: kniga zavlita* (In the Art Theater: the book of the literary director). Moscow: Vserossiiskoe teatral'noe obshchestvo (All-Russia Theater Society), 1976. Along with Markov's sympathetic portrayal of Bulgakov the playwright, contains important documents: minutes and resolutions of the Art Theater repertory committee.

Milne, Lesley. "M. A. Bulgakov and *Dead Souls:* The Problem of Adaptation." *Slavonic and East European Review* 52, no. 128 (July 1974):420–40. A well-documented study of Bulgakov's work on the adaptation of Gogol's novel; includes the text of the role of the Narrator which was later omitted from the Art Theater production.

Natov, Nadine. "Structural and Typological Ambivalence of Bulgakov's Novels Interpreted Against the Background of Baxtin's Theory of 'Grotesque Realism' and Carnivalization." In *American Contributions to the Eighth International Congress of Slavists,* 2:536–49. Columbus, Ohio: Slavica, 1978. Analyzes Bulgakov's craft in merging prosaic reality with a supernatural diabolic masquerade; studies sources and parallels for Bulgakov's demonology.

Pope, Richard W. F. "Ambiguity and Meaning in *The Master and Margarita:* The Role of Afranius." *Slavic Review* 36, no. 1 (March 1977):1–

24. An excellent study of the "ancient" chapters of the novel with emphasis on its plurisignificance and the importance of Afranius.

Proffer, Ellendea, ed. *Neizdannyi Bulgakov: Teksty i materialy* (Unpublished Bulgakov: texts and materials). Ann Arbor: Ardis, 1977. Includes first publication of Bulgakov's play *Batum,* records of the rehearsals of *A Cabal of Hypocrites,* and several letters and memoirs. Unfortunately contains no notes.

Proffer, Ellendea. "On *The Master and Margarita.*" In *Major Soviet Writers: Essays in Criticism,* edited by Edward J. Brown, 388–411. Oxford: Oxford University Press, 1973. Studies narrative techniques and recurrent symbols and points out differences in Bulgakov's attitudes toward polarities in moral concepts as compared to those that underlie Goethe's *Faust.*

Riggenbach, Heinrich. *Michail Bulgakovs Roman "Master i Margarita": Stil und Gestalt* (Bulgakov's novel *The Master and Margarita:* style and form). Bern: Peter Lang, 1979. The most detailed and comprehensive study of the novel's structure with emphasis on language and stylistic variety. Contains an extensive bibliography of works on *The Master and Margarita* in Slavic and West European languages up to 1978.

Russian Literature Triquarterly no. 15 (1978). Special issue edited by Carl R. and Ellendea Proffer. Translations of six of Bulgakov's short stories, the play *Last Days* (Pushkin), and three critical articles by Soviet scholars. Also includes six articles by American scholars dealing mostly with structural analysis of several of Bulgakov's works.

Utekhin, N. P. " 'Master i Margarita' M. Bulgakova: ob istochnikakh deistvitel'nykh i mnimykh" (M. Bulgakov's *The Master and Margarita:* on real and false sources). *Russkaia literatura* (Russian literature) (Leningrad), no. 4 (1979):89–109. A well-documented polemical article: the author objects to some views developed by Igor Belza in his article listed above.

Vilenkin, Vitalii. "O Mikhaile Afanas'eviche Bulgakove" (On M. A. Bulgakov). In *Vospominaniia s kommentariiami* (Memoirs with commentaries), 378–403. Moscow: Iskusstvo (Art), 1982. The author, a historian of the Moscow Art Theater, provides firsthand information about Bulgakov's relationship with the Art Theater and about the work on his plays.

Wright, A. Colin. *Mikhail Bulgakov: Life and Interpretation.* Toronto: University of Toronto Press, 1978. The first highly detailed study of Bulgakov's life in English. Depicts the hostile ambience in which Bulgakov's plays were produced quite thoroughly. Includes an extensive bibliography of works by and about Bulgakov. Indispensable for any student of Bulgakov.

Index